VISIBILITY

Success Stories from Elite Leaders Making an Impact from the Stage

DANNELLA BURNETT

HybridGlobal
PUBLISHING

Published by
Hybrid Global Publishing
301 E 57th Street
4th Floor
New York, NY 10022

Burnett, Dannella
      Visibility: Success Stories from Elite Leaders Making an Impact from the Stage
      LCCN: 2020922869
      ISBN: 978-1-951943-44-8
      eBook: 978-1-951943-45-5

Cover design by: Jonathan Pleska
Copyediting by: Claudia Volkman
Interior design by: Suba Murugan
Author photo by: Nikki Incandela Photography

www.speakersneedtospeak.com

CONTENTS

FOREWORD

They laughed at me in a very big way. I actually made quite a fool of myself standing in front of all those people making my presentation. They weren't laughing with me either; rather, they were laughing at me—and they laughed really loud too. It was an honest mistake, but it really threw me off.

I was speaking to one hundred-plus people at a mall in a Chamber of Commerce meeting-type setting. I was being somewhat introduced with an opportunity to share more about what I did at the time. I faced a big group that looked more like a crowd gathering around a street performer in New York City's Times Square.

I started to show them something I had invented as a multidimensional entrepreneur. I jokingly was about to say, "Yeah, I'm practically Howard Hughes," since this was right around the time the movie The Aviator came out with Leonardo DiCaprio playing Howard Hughes. But instead I said, "Yeah, I'm practically Hugh Hefner"—who, of course, was the famous founder of Playboy magazine.

So that was embarrassing. There are still people who remember this almost twenty years later. You'd think after that I'd never want to speak in front of a group again! I'd like to say that it was the only time I have messed up while delivering a message, but that isn't the case. The fact of the matter is that there are many things in the world that will discourage people like me and you from standing up and speaking out.

Being visible in general could go against your natural personality, the culture you live in, or even how you might interpret aspects of your religion. The idea to speak up, speak out, and share your professional expertise or personal beliefs can truly be quite controversial. Knowing when, how, what, why, and where you should lift up your voice can be puzzling even for the biggest celebrities, let alone the above-average authority of any particular industry.

Still, the idea to be truly heard and seen has never been more important. After all, you do not want to be the world's best-kept secret. You must make your presence felt if you are to leave your mark on the world, make a difference, and inspire action in individuals. That is the power of a speaker, an author, and a master mover of minds.

You can, in fact, learn to own and command a room with a soft voice. You have it in you to win over an audience of any size with nothing but your words. Your pitch, performance, and presentation can unlock the doors to every good thing you ever wanted for your world. Of course, none of this can be done without being visible, which means you can't reap the rewards of a listening audience without taking some risks of facing the haters in the crowd.

To be visible is everything. Publicity and public relations are a billion-dollar industry. Even the biggest names with the best on-screen personalities rely on publicists, speech writers, and scripts. Visibility is so important; as the saying goes, "There is no such thing as bad press." As a writer, a speaker, a former CEO of Guerrilla Marketing, and a Beverly Hills publicist, I can tell you firsthand that there are people not only willing to be sued but even hoping to be sued over something just so they would be featured in the mainstream media.

Your optics—the way people see you and your visibility—can contribute to your perceived relevance in the world. I know it's crazy, and like me, you might hate that fact, but you should also consider (as I do) that you are better to play the game than to try to change it. To have a platform, an audience, and a following and to be seen regularly is a truly powerful opportunity to do some good in the world.

This book shares the keys to speaking up, speaking out, and finding victory through strategic visibility. The authors you'll be introduced to in these pages are taking calculated risks, making strategic moves, and making a living speaking from their hearts. You might call them the difference makers or truth tellers of their industries.

Whether you want to reach the unreachable, influence the affluent, or even heal the hurting in a big way, you can't afford to be the world's best-kept secret. You must take massive amounts of action and put in the work that will eventually win over the hearts and heads of every audience.

You will have to be teachable at all hours and willing to be uncomfortable at times. You will have to accept the fact that there will be people who will try to tear you down as you build yourself up. You have to learn to love people underestimating you and use it to fire up your focus and master your message.

This book will help you with all of this and so much more. Keep reading! Keep going, perfect your presentations, find your people, develop your God-given talents, and fulfill your purpose through your visibility.

David T. Fagan, Award-Winning, Media-Celebrated
www.davidtfagan.com

SHARE YOUR MESSAGE!
BE A LEADER! GET ON STAGE!
BE A SPEAKER!

DANNELLA BURNETT

The call to speak has been shouted from the rooftops, shared in workshops, and discussed in coaching sessions for years, and it has only gotten louder. In March 2020 there were an estimated forty thousand professional speakers in the United States alone, and they were generating 1.9 billion dollars in annual revenue. This is income generated by speaking fees as well as books, courses, programs, products, and coaching services. As the industry grew, more and more business owners, coaches, and marketers entered the speaking world and stepped onto these stages to share messages of business, health and wellness, personal development, and more.

But even with all those speakers, there are still more opportunities that remain unfilled.

Prior to March 2020, it was estimated that there were more than seven thousand speaking opportunities EVERY DAY in the United States. These ranged from smaller networking events and company workshops to larger conferences, expos, corporate trainings, nonprofit fundraisers, and more. Now at the end of 2020 and with all the changes that have taken place as events and speaking opportunities have gone virtual, it's actually estimated that there could be eight to ten times that number of opportunities. There is an abundance of speaking opportunities; however, many speakers still struggle with how to get on stages and share their messages of inspiration, education, motivation, monetization, or transformation.

Many of them struggle with how to take advantage of the speed of events and speaking opportunities now available in the virtual world.

As an event producer for the last thirty years—and especially for the last eight years at the national level with five, six, and seven-figure expert events, I've helped connect many speakers with high-level, lucrative speaking opportunities. My team and I look for ways to make a match that creates the win-win-win for the event host, the speaker, and the attendees. When speakers are in front of the right audience in the right environment and bring their right self to the mic . . . MAGIC!

Getting visibility and sharing your message is important; as a speaker, you need to speak, but you also need to get paid. Many of the speakers I've met are so passionate about their message, have a huge desire to serve, help others overcome, and want to change the world, but they forget that speaking is a business. There has to be a strategy to make money so the message can grow and the speaker can keep speaking!

There are a few key pathways for getting paid and a few options within each path. All are great, viable options, and all have their own unique challenges and benefits. The first is *keynote speaking* (being paid to speak). This is a good for a motivational, inspirational, or educational speaker. There is often an application process, and the speaker must show the value not only for the audience, but for the entity that is writing the check. Frequently this is a corporation, a university, a nonprofit organization, or an association that is hiring a keynote speaker for an annual conference, workshop, or other event for their members or employees. This type of speaking definitely has the most competition, and the payoff is getting the payment for the talk. You may be able to negotiate including books sales in the deal, but frequently you are not able to promote the rest of your business, such as courses or coaching.

The second pathway for speaking is *sponsorship speaking* (paying to speak). Here the speaker pays for the opportunity to speak. If you are a speaker who is just starting out, this may seem counterintuitive, but many seasoned speakers prefer this speaking pathway. While you need to be able to discern the right sponsorships for you, this can be the fastest path to growing your list, selling from the stage, and filling your business courses and programs. It can be far more profitable than getting paid to speak. Sponsorships can range from a few hundred dollars to tens of thousands of dollars, so understanding how you are going to use that speaking opportunity to lead to business is critical.

The third pathway is *speaking for free*. In this case, no money changes hands, but there may be a requirement to promote the event, a swap of speaking opportunities, or a similar trade of value. This can be the best option for gathering contacts, scheduling follow-up consulting or coaching calls, and getting exposure to new audiences. In this case, the speaker often offers a complimentary consultation or strategy call, an ebook, an assessment, or some other content in exchange for the audience's contact information.

This type of speaking has literally exploded in the virtual world, giving many speakers incredible opportunities to gain visibility, make new connections, and increase influence in their industries. Keynotes, on the other hand, have become a more difficult pathway to get consistent and profitable speaking opportunities. More corporate and organizational events have been postponed or are harder to locate as decision makers are working from home and may not be creating as many opportunities for paid speaking gigs. Sponsorships continue to be a very viable option as long as the speaker does due diligence on the audience, the opportunity, and the ability to get a return on their investment.

Another great option for speakers to get visibility is something that previously hasn't been seen as similar in status: being featured as a guest on podcasts, social media live events, radio, or livestream TV. Social media interviews are really good opportunities for speakers—they are frequently free opportunities and provide great exposure and new connections.

Up to this point, I've highlighted ways for speakers to gain visibility by leveraging other platforms—events, summits, and podcasts created by others that allow a speaker to share with a large audience and thus grow their audience, connections, and business. But social media is also a great environment for speakers to create their own platform for exposure. Virtual events are more economical to produce because they are without the expenses of venue and hospitality, and it's much easier to invite larger and more diverse audiences. There may be more needs in the areas of technology and team, but overall it's still easier to launch a virtual event, podcast, or social media "program" than ever with the right support and strategies.

There are many types of events, from short workshops to one to three-day enrollment events, retreats, and more. Knowing what strategies to apply to the different types of events can help business owners easily fill their programs, courses, and coaching groups.

As we move further into the virtual world and experiment with hybrid events while eventually seeing more in-person stages come back to the forefront, it will be interesting to find new ways to support speakers and event clients so they get the visibility and monetization they need to grow businesses and make an impact. By keeping the main thing the main thing and understanding the needs of events, speakers, and audiences, I'm confident that the best opportunities will continue to present themselves for our clients and our own businesses.

I'm also confident that experts, entrepreneurs, and coaches will continue to use speaking as the fastest path to clients, influence, and connection. In this fast-paced virtual world, as we transition to hybrid and back to in-person events, it will be even more important for speakers to get support—such as our Speakers Need To Speak services—to help them navigate quickly and systematically. 2020 has been a very interesting year as we've found new ways to gain the needed visibility to grow and scale businesses, and many of the lessons learned will stay with us for years to come. I'm excited to see how the event and speaking industries will continue to grow and adapt and how experts will continue to expand their influence and make bigger and bigger impacts on individuals and the world.

Owner of Encore Elite Events & Speakers Need To Speak, **Dannella** is a creative force with a passion for connecting experts to those they serve through speaking & events while generating profitable visibility! Through her connections millions of dollars have been generated and tens of thousands of lives impacted through live events!

www.speakersneedtospeak.com

FROM VICTIM TO SURVIVOR AND BEYOND

DR. LORI BETH BISBEY

When I was nine years old, I made myself a bottle to live in as I waited for my Master like Jeannie on *I Dream of Jeannie*. I already knew what turned me on sexually. That isn't strange—most people have an idea of their sexuality by then; we just don't usually identify that this is the case unless we are not heterosexual. I understood that my desires were different from the desires my friends had. In high school when we were all dating, I really understood how different my desires were. I wanted to be overpowered, to surrender. I had shame around my desires, but I didn't know what to do about that.

I learned very young that being in control was a way to limit the amount of pain (both emotional and physical) we experience in life. Being in control is a positive thing in most areas of life. But being aggressively in control makes sex and relationships extremely difficult. Orgasm requires a letting go of control. Relationships require trust, and that requires a letting go of control as well.

When I was nineteen, I met Damien. He was everything I believed I wanted, and he didn't think my desires were strange. He had complementary desires. At nineteen, I thought I had found my soul mate. I decided then that I would surrender to him; I would give up control. This was an enormous risk for me, but I was sure that he was the One.

The first period of time we were together was perfect, and then one day he turned into a monster. He held me captive for five days, and during that time, he beat me and raped me repeatedly. He choked me until I died. I came back to life with him pounding on my chest and giving me mouth-to-mouth resuscitation.

I was devastated by this experience. I developed post-traumatic stress disorder (PTSD). I was constantly anxious; I had flashbacks and intrusive thoughts. I tried to regain control in my life, and this led to me to be even more of a control freak.

I felt tremendous shame about my desires, and my relationships suffered. Because I could not accept my desires or myself, my relationship choices were abysmal. I chose people who were emotionally unavailable, who had substance abuse issues, and who also had PTSD. These relationships didn't work and only left me feeling worse and like I needed to hold even tighter to control.

When I went to university, I studied broadcast journalism. I love to write and to be on stage. I wanted to use both my writing skills and my love of entertaining, and journalism seemed the best way to do this. After Damien, though, it didn't make sense anymore. I switched to psychology and began training as a psychologist. I started in therapy soon after being held captive by Damien. For the first few years, therapy kept me stable and able to continue my training.

Then I accessed therapy specific to PTSD, and this was amazing. I no longer had any symptoms. I no longer felt like a victim or even like a survivor. I had my life back—with one exception. My relationships were still a mess. I couldn't trust fully in a relationship. I couldn't surrender, and so pleasure was extremely difficult.

I began helping other trauma survivors to get their lives back. I spoke in front of audiences about moving from victim to survivor and then beyond. I worked with clients using Traumatic Incident Reduction, the amazing treatment that helped me. I did research on treatment for crime victims with post-traumatic stress disorder. I taught therapists how to use this treatment and ultimately co-authored a book in 1998 on PTSD that focused on this treatment method.

At the same time, I looked for a way to deal with the shame that still remained around my desires and my inability to give up any control. I was actively working with couples and individuals on sex and relationships. Many of the women I worked with had experienced sexual violence and also had difficulty with their sexual relationships. I started trying a variety of methods of therapy, coaching, and spiritual practice in an effort to get rid of the persistent shame I felt. Eventually, a combination of experiential and reflective practices worked.

The most important lesson I learned through this process is that surrender is the key to me being in flow. When I am in flow, I am on purpose, and all things come easily to me. When I hold tight to control, things become difficult. For me, surrender is a spiritual concept as well as integrated into my relationships. I surrender to a power higher than myself, and I surrender to that part of myself that works in my best interests.

After integrating my experiences and finally becoming comfortable with my own sexual desires, I started working with my therapy and coaching clients to help them to experience the same results. Once my shame was gone, I began to shine. I finally had exciting and satisfying sexual relationships, and this made an incredible impact on my other relationships too.

I met my husband in 2009, and we have been happily together ever since. Our relationship is the first one I have had with someone who sees and loves all of me and with whom I have never felt shame. Our relationship suits us both and allows us both to live fully and out loud.

I work with clients using my unique combination of talents to help them create and maintain meaningful relationships that have sizzling sex without shame. I teach emotional, social, and relationship skills that bring them to their authentic expressions of self and through that to their most authentic relationships. I specialize in working with people who have gender, sex, and relationship diversities. I provide a judgment-free, shame-free space and the tools they need to create the relationship styles that bring them the most pleasure, joy, and love.

Being authentic and without shame, I have more energy, and I bring this energy to everything I do. I returned to broadcasting by starting a podcast, The A to Z of Sex®, in 2016 and started presenting regularly on stages of all sizes. The authentic energy I now feel allows me to reach more people through my writing, podcasting, and speaking. Speaking has allowed me to touch people directly in a larger group and to give them tools to create change.

The more integrated you are, the more energy you bring to all you do. If you are carrying shame about any part of yourself or your life, this is communicated everywhere in your life. People feel it as a point of disconnection and then find it hard to believe and/or relate to your message. When there is authenticity, there is no disconnect, and you bring your full energy and attention to everything. The power of your message is exponentially increased as a result. You shine, and people are drawn to your energy.

My present life is incredible. I wake up each day knowing I am where I need to be, doing what I need to do. I have a daily practice that helps me to stay on my path. I was reborn at nineteen, though I did not realize it at the time. Now at fifty-seven, I greet each day in the knowledge that I have been gifted this time and that surrender allows me to use that time to the fullest.

Dr. Lori Beth Bisbey is a psychologist, sex and intimacy coach, author, podcast host, and speaker who has been helping people for over thirty years to create and maintain meaningful relationships with sizzling sex (and without shame). Dr. Bisbey hosts The A to Z of Sex® podcast.

www.drloribethbisbey.com

A PICTURE IS WORTH A THOUSAND WORDS

BRIGETTE CALLAHAN

I was in fifth grade when we moved to the middle of the US. I was born and raised in California, and I knew I was not in my element. During this time I discovered I loved drawing. It was my escape, and I received continuous acknowledgments from my mother. But my stepfather would tell me, "You'll never make money as an artist." That devastated me.

My stepfather was a very successful salesman when we moved to Nebraska for his career. My mom gave a dinner party one night to the high-level executives of his company. My stepfather called me in to the living room and said, "This is the vice-president of marketing, and I thought you'd want to know what it would be like to work in their art department." All I could say was "I don't want to draw doorknobs all day." They roared with laughter, and I ran to my bedroom, embarrassed.

It was clear that my stepfather didn't care about what I wanted and didn't understand my passion. I grew up wanting to prove him wrong; I wanted to show him that I could be a successful artist.

After graduating from college with a degree in fine art, I got a job working as a graphic designer for an automotive aftermarket manufacturer. I loved that job. I learned so much in two years and was able to buy a brand-new car with my salary. I was on the road to making it.

Next I moved to San Diego and began working for a multimedia company. I had no idea what they did. I was hired to be the assistant to the art director, and my job was to make his storyboards a reality from an art perspective.

One of my first assignments was to take a globe and paint the land black and the water white. I had the weekend to finish it. I had no idea why I was doing this; I just knew I had to do a great job. Come Monday, my boss asked if I completed the task. I said, "Yes!" and showed him. He was happy and asked me to run it over to the photo studio down the hall. I thought, *Wow, you have your own photo studio? Awesome.*

I handed it to the photographer, and he took the globe and put it on a tripod with a spindle which allowed him to rotate it and take twelve still images. A couple of days later, I was working at my drawing table and heard loud music. I asked my boss, "What is that?" He said it was the producer programming a show for a company called NCR, and he asked if I wanted to go down to the theatre to watch. Like a little kid, I said, "YES," and he took me down there. I saw a large, panoramic screen, the size of a billboard, in a dark, smaller-sized theatre. The music welled up, and the black screen slowly faded to an image of a globe rotating. The colors were brilliant blue and green gradations. It was amazing. "I created that artwork!" I said to myself, feeling like I worked in Hollywood.

This was the beginning of my career designing slideshows. I never knew it would create a lifelong passion of working with speakers and being committed to giving the audience what they truly desire: an experience of entertainment and education similar to watching a TV show or seeing a Hollywood movie.

We've all experienced the boring slideshow. And most of us have experienced it more than we'd like to. Yet as speakers, if we create our own slides, we think these are going to be fine. We don't get the connection that we are doing the same thing: creating a boring presentation. I call this the "undeclared slide shame." We all have it. But we don't want to face it. And we don't know what to do to make it better.

Most people realize when they meet me that they've never heard of someone doing what I do for a living. That intrigues me because it's simply my passion. I'm committed to abolishing the boring slide and creating a win-win experience for the speaker and the audience. I want the audience to feel appreciated and respected and ultimately glad they came. And there's this unconscious sense that when slides are revealed and they are well made, the audience feels a connection to the speaker and wants to pay attention and listen keenly. They are fascinated and can't wait for what's next. This experience creates the "WOW factor." And ultimately it creates better results.

One of the most shocking realizations I share with speakers is that if you want to put your audience to sleep, design all your slides on a white background. Every time I say this, they give me a look of horror because most people design their slides this way, thinking that's the way to go. They don't realize how that impacts the brain.

When looking at projected light such as a television screen or a slide projector, our eyes go to the light, unlike when we look at reflected light like a printed brochure with text and pictures. If we are looking at a white background with a bunch of dark text, our brain has to conjugate the light and the dark. We look at each letter, trying to formulate what letter it is and then we formulate the word . . . and then we formulate the sentence. All this brainpower overwhelms us to the point that after about five or ten minutes, we're toast. We can't listen anymore . . . and we just tune out the speaker.

I equate a white slide background with dark text as a similar experience to being in a movie theater when you've got our popcorn, have just finished watching the trailers, and the movie starts. And if no one turn the lights off, you're like, "OK, the movie started—can you turn the lights down, please?" The white background is like a blinding flashlight in our eyes, and this creates the ultimate uncomfortable feeling.

Another issue is that most speakers feel the need to read what's written on the slides to the audience. Who wants to watch a movie with subtitles? Not me. So why would someone want to see a slideshow with a bunch of text?

This kind of slide presentation is the amateur way to go, and it doesn't generate the results the speaker is expecting. From my professional background, it's better to start out with a storyboard of the elements you want to convey. I like to think of it as stringing stories together. Then you can add images that could portray those stories well.

You might start with a full-screen, edge-to-edge image, and if the image is compelling enough, that's all you need. Just tell your story, and as you're sharing your story, the audience is looking at the image. They are formulating a memory of what they hear coupled with what they see, and this memory becomes ten times more impactful on their brain than if they're seeing text and listening to someone reading it. A picture really is worth a thousand words. As speakers we all want to be remembered, and we want what we are conveying to be remembered for a long time too.

What fascinates me is always looking for new ways to convey visual imagery that's impactful. When I watch TV or see movies, I get ideas to visually compel and engage in ways that are fresh and different. When I get to present these distinctions to an audience, I always get an engaged crowd. I show them before-and-after slides, and they are struck by how different things can look. It's my life work; it's what I love to do.

My commitment is to make a difference for one million audience members by working with one thousand speakers.

Brigette Callahan has been a slide-presentation designer for more than thirty years. She has worked with some of the biggest names in business, including Xerox, Acura, Samsung, and PayPal. She is passionate about helping speakers create presentations that engage and inspire their audience, turning them into raving fans.

www.presentationdesignexpert.com/visibility

SPEAK YOUR WAY TO OVER 100K

JEN COFFEL

Speaking is the most powerful lead source and revenue-generating machine for any entrepreneur who knows their core genius and creates a strategically designed talk around it. Do you know your core genius? If you know your core genius and you build your business core profits around your core genius, you can speak your way to over 100K! And when I say speak your way to over 100K, I mean that you can do that in just one talk!

Identifying your core genius is absolutely the most important critical first step to designing a signature talk that will highlight your expertise, attract your ideal clients, and turn your business into a revenue-generating machine.

Let's break down the words *core genius*. When you think of the word *core*, what comes to mind? I think about what God created me to do. What did God create you to do? What do you think about when you think of the word *genius*? I think your genius is what you've become an expert in and what you have studied. So if you combine what you were created for—your core—along with the expert study that you've done—your genius—that becomes your core genius!

It's really hard to identify your core genius for yourself. And the reason it's hard is that it's so much a part of who you are. In fact, the work you do in your core genius comes so easy for you that you don't even think it's that special because it's just how you are. It's how you think. It's your unique perspective. It's what you do measurably better than others. It's what makes you so special.

Your core genius needs to be at the center of your branding, your messaging, your core business profit centers, and especially your signature talk.

I believe that helping entrepreneurs identify their core genius is *my* core genius! When I do this with my clients, I usually get three reactions:

1. They start to cry because finally they feel they have a way to really explain what they do and what makes them special and unique.
2. They start to laugh because they get so excited about their confusion going away, and they can see clearly how to apply all the various strategies they are pursuing and learning to their business.
3. They look me in the eyes and calmly and confidently say "YES! YES! YES!" as their heads nod up and down, with a look in their eyes of total peace and a knowing that they now have unlocked the missing piece that they needed to soar in their business.

Samantha, a psychotherapist, was one of my clients who started laughing when I helped her discover her core genius. When we began working together, she shared with me that she really loved helping women put an end to anxiety. She said her colleagues actually criticized her and said that it wasn't possible to put an end to anxiety. They believe that psychotherapists can only teach people to cope with anxiety. Samantha knew she could put an end to anxiety, but she never considered focusing on this target market. She was treating every type of mental health challenge: divorce, depression, grief, anxiety, etc. The idea of focusing on her core genius and creating a full caseload of clients that matched her core genius was super exciting to her. After working together to design her signature talk to attract clients with anxiety, Samantha had the opportunity to speak in front of 150 women. She only had room on her calendar to offer eight consults. As Samantha was finishing her talk and making her offer, she watched women lining up at her table in the back of the room, and all eight spots were filled before she got off the stage. She had a waiting list over twenty people willing to wait to work with her. The demand for Samantha's services became so overwhelmingly successful that she had to create a whole new brand called Dare To End Anxiety that included on-demand courses so she could serve more people. She went from making 3K a month to over 10K a month in just five months through the power of speaking around her core genius. Samantha knows what is feels like to Speak Your Way to Over 100K!

Now that you know the core genius foundation needed to speak your way to over 100K, let's dive into what every entrepreneur that wants to use speaking as a revenue-generating machine will need to implement. I call this the 10x Advantage: 8 Pillars to Profitable Speaking.

Pillar #1 – Tantalizing Titles: Personalize signature talk titles to speak to your top three markets consisting of your ideal clients. Titles with a great hook will get you booked. In fact, you can use the same exact signature talk for all three titles. You may need to tweak the talk slightly based on the target market, but when your talk is built around your core genius, then you can essentially share the same message, framing it for a specific target market.

Pillar #2 – Origin Story: Craft your unique personal transformation story to build trust, show authenticity, and connect with your audience. Stories are not a series of events. There are stages to a story, and learning to tell your story is the fastest path to having your ideal client get to know, like, and trust you. People love stories that move them emotionally.

Pillar #3 – Heal the Headache: Design your talk for your ideal client, address their biggest problems, and offer your unparalleled solution.

Pillar #4 – Powerful Principles: Strategically design signature talk content that highlights your expertise, attracts your ideal clients, and leaves them wanting more. These principles need to be packed with amazing stories. Stories inspire and cause audiences to remember you. Stories and inspiration (not information) create a line of people wanting to speak with you. Be inspirational, not informational.

Pillar #5 – Lead Magnet: Learn to create and utilize the perfect freebie to grow your email/contact database for ongoing sales and huge future revenue.

Pillar #6 – Art of the Offer: Create a compelling paid offer or free gift offer that your ideal client cannot resist! The most effective offer is a free consultation that is essentially a sales conversation. But the key to creating a compelling offer is naming the offer. For example, the name of one of my offers is a "Speak Your Way to Over 100K session." Tie the offer name to the ultimate result your ideal client wants.

Pillar #7 – Talk Takeaways: The ideal copy to give meeting planners to fill every seat in the room. This is not a description of your talk. It is copy that will make people curious and want to come to your talk to learn more.

Pillar #8 – Get Booked Bio: Your new speaker bio will show meeting planners and event promoters that you are a top speaker! Prestige, credibility, and expertise all in one place will get you booked nearly anywhere.

In conclusion, there is no faster path to Speaking Your Way to Over 100k than first identifying your core genius! And I have found there is no faster path to profits in business than speaking. I love Mark Twain's quote, "The two most important days of your life are the day you are born and the day you find out why."

If discovering your core genius and using speaking to grow your business to over 100K is something that interests you, I would love to talk with you! To make the most of our time together on the phone, please visit www.JenCoffel.com/breakthrough so I can get to know you and your business. When you complete the questionnaire, I will send you a link to schedule a Speak Your Way to Over 100K session.

Jen Coffel is CEO of Engaging Speakers, a successful business coach, a bestselling author with four books, and a philanthropist. With two decades of business experience, Jen built her first four businesses to six figures each, all in under a year and all in different industries. But she is most proud of founding her own international nonprofit, Handing Hope, which brings comfort and smiles to children battling cancer in twelve states and three countries around the world.

www.jencoffel.com

CREATING A LEGACY

JUDY L. COPENBARGER, JD, CFP®, AIF®

I could barely see beyond the edges of the backstage décor and into the fog of the bright stage and laser lights. Tossing my hair back one more time and smoothing my skirt for any last-minute wrinkles, I was ready.

It was a familiar feeling to be strolling onstage slightly blinded, yet I was clearer than ever about what the next hour would bring.

Because I could only see the halo of light around the MC introducing me and I could barely make out the edge of the high stage, it was time to rely upon my sense of hearing—so I listened.

"Ladies and gentlemen, prepare yourselves for the next minutes as you become more educated, inspired, restored, and confident than ever before . . . that YOU . . . can master your money, optimize your relationships, increase your business, and secure your future with what you are soon to learn from our own phenomenal, life-changing, over-the-top strategic financial planner . . . known as 'the money-whisperer,' 'fiduciary extraordinaire,' 'attorney and financial strategist,' Dr. Judy Copenbarger!"

[thunderous applause]

I reflect on this collection of speaking memories with a smile, acknowledging my good fortune to have discovered and uncovered my legacy early in life. I was born to teach, to inspire, to lead, to train. I knew this as a child, but exactly who was supposed to be the recipient of my work?

The answer has unfolded throughout the years. In school, college, and graduate school, I taught my peers, then it was our five children, friends in our inner circle, clients, like-minded colleagues, those involved in activities and causes that I care about, and leaders and world-changers.

When it comes down to it, everything I have learned and passed on to others is grounded in communication. Regardless with whom I am working, the concept, processes, and information are all the same.

Simply put, it takes communication to get this done!

In my professional life as an estate planning and strategic financial planning expert, I found myself helping others to generate wealth, optimize their lifestyle, structure their organization, and create their legacy.

In every stage, the key has been—and still is—communication.

Let's take a look at an excerpt from chapter nine, "The Elements of Mastery" from *Money Truth & Life*:

MASTERING COMMUNICATION

In order to master communication (or anything else), you need three elements. If any of the elements is missing, you can still achieve a moderate level of success, but that's it. Don't settle! In order to reach your potential and attain goals beyond your expectations, you will need mastery. Here are the three necessary elements for mastery: Knowledge, Resources, and Motivation.

1. Knowledge

This is your "know-how." You will need to have an understanding of basic information. For a concert pianist to master his craft, he needs to know something about music.

As a small child, Theodore spent hours each day swinging his legs below the piano bench as he sat and picked away at the black-and-white keys. He learned music theory, how to count out the timing, how to harmonize the notes, and precisely how to use his foot pedals, arms, and fingers to bring the music on each page to life.

In college, he learned even more about piano technique, music genres, and the business of being a touring world-class pianist.

He could not have enjoyed success without the know-how of music, piano technique, business, and the art of performing.

2. Resources

This is your "need it." You will need resources in order to master whatever you put your mind to. You need resources to master a business. Perhaps you will need funding, equipment, good ideas, or personnel.

You need resources for a world-class mountain climb. Perhaps you will need a support team, transportation, appropriate climbing gear and attire, and optimal hydration and nutrition elements.

At some point, Theodore, our world-class concert pianist, would have to have access to music, talented musicians to support his performances, and a stage. Imagine if he showed up onstage to play and had to stop to plug in his keyboard first. A grand piano is a necessary resource for his success.

3. Motivation

This is your "want to." It doesn't matter how much you know and how equipped you are; you won't take action if you are not inspired. The third necessary element to mastery requires that you actually want to put in the effort to succeed.

Without motivation from the heart, it will be impossible to attain and sustain a successful mastery. So are you willing to actually do what it takes to get to the finish line?

To become profitable in your business, are you ready to withstand the expenses, setbacks, time constraints, fear, and negativity from your competitors? Do you have the motivation to break through when you want to break down?

To climb that mountain, are you willing to train your body, calendar the time for travel, and incur the expenses necessary to complete your journey to the summit? When it seems hopeless, do you have the motivation to remain hopeful and push on?

There were many times while sitting on that piano bench that Theodore wanted to walk away from those keys and never return. When he could hear the other children playing ball outside through the window near the piano where he practiced, his motivation to be the greatest pianist onstage kept him at the piano.

When Theodore considered the extreme expense of his advanced musical degrees, his desire kept him committed. At times, he thought he would never attain the bookings or be invited to perform in specific venues, but his desire and commitment to his dream gave him the motivation to stay on track until he was performing on the largest world stages with the most talented musicians.

You will also master whatever you choose by gaining knowledge, obtaining resources, and sustaining motivation.

My journey has included financial planning, parenting five children (including twins), law school, business and taxation expertise, and serving clients as a strategic planner and fiduciary.

Throughout the years, I have experienced "organic growth," creating relationships and growing several businesses to substantial levels. Interviewers, influencers, colleagues, and clients often ask how I grew such substantial businesses and became a popular renowned speaker, author, educator, parent, and thought leader. It was through communication.

The journey, until very recently, has been solely nose-to-nose and knee-to-knee, simple word-of-mouth communication, and referrals.

Without a team of SEO optimizers, client acquisition planning teams, marketing strategies, and bottomless budgets, I've done what I knew to do: just communicate.

Here's the good news for you. It's not a nose-to-nose and knee-to-knee world anymore. In this new world, we don't have to be anywhere in particular, on any given day, or on any specific stage.

While coaching and mentoring professionals, business owners, and ministry leaders, I am often asked how to successfully build an ideal community of "clients." I say, "Just be where 'they' are." Well, where they are currently is online. Our world has changed.

My own experience of "being where they are" has transitioned through the years. I've led legal events where we worked with judges and attorneys through MCLE training and philanthropic endeavors. When our children came along, the groups at MOPS and MOMS groups, churches, and parenting groups were added. As a financial planner, my audience has become financial, taxation, banking, and real estate professionals. Later, my academia audience expanded to include universities and leaders of ministries and pastors via seminars, workshops, and boardroom trainings. In our day-to-day business dealings, we've served wealthy families and closely held family businesses through retreats, business development, and legacy planning summits.

Recently, virtual workshops, podcasts, conferences, summits, and television and radio interviews have replaced the need to personally "be there." Although I will always prefer seeing people face-to-face, my legacy is able to expand to reach well beyond my expectations in this new world. I embrace the new normal.

I am grateful for all the opportunities, lifestyle, family growth, and impact on lives of others. I am thankful for the teams of virtual experts that connect with my message and propel it forward. I honor those who have been seeking the truth about money and have finally found it. This is what I was born to do.

My legacy is expressed as the Money Truth & Life Online Mastery Course where families and small business owners find financial wisdom. In the simple video series of this program, all critical elements of finance are presented: taxation, investments, legacy and legal entities, banking, cash flows and cash reserves, and insurance.

I am blessed to have had many platforms to impact the lives of others—from classrooms to offices, from boardrooms to ballrooms. This is my stage.

And before fading into the bright backstage lighting, my voice cracks just a little as I articulate this.

" . . . and my intention is that you leave here touched, moved, and inspired to gain traction, move forward, and master your next level of life, family, business, and purpose. This is the gift I give to you. Enjoy your journey."

Yes, this is my legacy.

Judy L. Copenbarger, JD, CFP®, AIF®, founded The Complete MONEY TRUTH & LIFE Online Mastery Program so families worldwide can access practical wisdom for life. President of Copenbarger Corporation in Newport Beach, California, Judy is a bestselling author, experienced strategic financial and estate planner, wife, farmer, and "mom" to five world changers.

www.judycopenbarger.com/truth

YOUR VOICE IS YOUR TICKET TO GREAT THINGS!

MOIRA NÍ GHALLACHÓIR

Growing up in Scotland, and then Donegal in Ireland, my only memories of school are getting in trouble for talking too much. I grew up with a clear message of "You can show up, you can be seen, but you cannot be heard—and if you are, there will be consequences . . ."

By the age of ten, I believed that I was cursed for always talking too much.

When I went to high school, it seemed that I was always in trouble, not just with the teachers, but with my friends as well. Every time I wanted to share my opinion, I was either shunned by my friends or told to get out of the classroom by my teachers.

I started to become known as "the one who talked too much."

I remember one day standing outside my classroom door because I was in trouble again for talking, I heard another teacher coming down the corridor, I tried to hide myself in the doorway so she wouldn't see me . . . but she did anyway.

"Outside again for talking too much?" she said. "You know, you're not going to get very far, Moira, if all you want to do is talk all the time."

I remember feeling so ashamed and embarrassed, and I wondered if she was right—maybe I wasn't going to make anything of my life.

But one of the BEST decisions I ever made was NOT to listen to those teachers and instead listen to the voice inside my own head. The one that was literally shouting, "Your voice is your ticket to great things!"

Fast-forward to today, and I now travel the world as an international speaker. I've built a multiple six-figure business speaking in exotic locations around the world because I realized that speaking wasn't my biggest curse—it was my biggest gift. And now I help other entrepreneurs make that same discovery.

I followed some simple rules to get to where I am today. But those rules have changed in this new, ultra-fast-moving virtual world. I'll share those new rules with you so you can have the impact and success you want from speaking.

You see, I believe in my heart that more women need to speak, need to be heard, and need to dissolve any voices from their past that keep them from unleashing their unique voice. I believe that more women can build a dynamic business that makes a massive impact in the world—from the stage.

The world is different right now, and the opportunity for speakers in the virtual world is more than exponential. YOU can have a space in that.

Your voice can play a massive part in helping you get more visibility, be seen as an expert, and create the impact and the success you dream of as an entrepreneur.

You may not have ever thought about being a speaker, but as an entrepreneur, you are likely dreaming of enrolling more clients, making more money, and having the kind of lifestyle that a successful business can give you, right?

I know I certainly was. But I just didn't jump on a big stage and everything fell into place. No, I found lots and lots of small stages, and I honestly believe I failed my way to where I am today. Those are the rules that I followed.

Today there are new rules, and you don't even have to travel. You can start from anywhere because there are no limitations about where you can speak. In fact, you're surrounded by speaking opportunities, but you're just not asking for them.

Today there are new rules for connecting and getting clients. I'll share three of those with you that will help you get more visibility and make a bigger impact as a speaker.

1. Amplify You.

As an entrepreneur and a speaker, you're creating a persona, and you want to amplify the things about you that are most magnetic. For example, I love to travel, I love adventure, I love making money, and I love doing all things with style and flair. And so I've created my business around all of those things.

Did I know this when I started out? No. But I learned how my business could help me have the life I dreamed, and it evolved with me.

When you amplify who you are, you attract people that resonate with you and want to follow you. They want to be inspired by your journey, your story, your experience, and your highs and lows—just as you want what you see in the thought leaders and speakers you follow.

2. Invite Your Perfect Audience.

Gone are the days of traveling to events and hoping to meet the people you want to meet in places that took you hours to get to. In this virtual world we're in, you can literally invite your own perfect audience. The volume and quality of the people we now have access to in our networks is through the roof, and you can literally invite your perfect audience to your event.

Your conversion rate will go up when the people you invite are already in alignment with you. This way you're not throwing something at the wall and hoping it sticks, which unfortunately is what most people are doing. When you invite your perfect audience, it's like you're throwing something that's already got adhesive on it so you're sure it will stick!

3. Add a Layer of Engagement.

These days you need to add a whole other layer of engagement to your presentations. Yes, you can make money with webinars, but you can really stand out by adding a layer of engagement to the way you present those webinars. You can make an offer using slides, but you'll also just look like everyone else doing similar online presentations.

What you need is to create more experience, not merely share more information. Presenting information is the old way. The new way is making your presentations more of an experience where you take your audience on a journey with you. If you can create an experience, the information you share will stick, and people will leave your presentation wanting more.

I'll share a perfect example of how experience can compound the impact and attract the perfect audience.

Late last year I was in Paris for my private clients' retreat, and I had an evening to spare. And because I love networking, I was looking for a cool event I could attend. I had one goal in mind: I wanted to meet some like-minded female entrepreneurs and make some real connections. But I couldn't find anything other than the same old stuffy, stiff networking events.

So I decided to create my own. You see, I believe entrepreneurs deserve events that are not just about rehearsed intros and awkward conversations. We deserve real, deep meaningful connections—authentic conversations that allow us to share what's most important to us.

I found a trendy bar with a back room I could use. And with the few contacts I had in Paris at that time, I was able to invite twenty-three women entrepreneurs to come to my secret, supper-style event.

What was born on that amazing evening was a revolutionary idea: Secret Suppers Worldwide™. These are exclusive, one-of-a-kind, supper-style gatherings where business owners can connect with other dynamic business owners who are up to big things in the world.

I moved to Bali, and I hosted another event there. Then, when the whole COVID thing hit, I recreated my Secret Suppers Worldwide online. And I've been filling these intimate gatherings every month since. And when the pandemic lifts and the world can breathe again, I will be globe-trotting around the world in fabulous shoes, parachuting into exciting cities, and hosting these one-of-a-kind events for entrepreneurs.

And the best part? Ten percent of all the revenue that's generated goes to giving micro business loans to women in third-world countries. My goal for 2021 is to impact five hundred women with Secret Suppers Worldwide™.

It's hard to believe I was ten thousand dollars in debt when I did my first speaking gig. Just three years later, I had closed half a million in revenue from speaking. I thought that was fast, but with the way the virtual world is right now and the potential for visibility, with focus and determination you could do this even faster.

Speaking has changed me and my life in so many ways. I have the opportunity to speak worldwide, and I get to enjoy lots of freedom and adventure. You can have this, too, if you just follow these three new rules. Amplifying you and inviting your perfect audience will get you started—and adding a layer of engagement will take your business through the roof and around the world!

Moira Ní Ghallachóir shows female entrepreneurs a powerful pathway to building a top-tier income and a globe-trotting lifestyle from speaking live and virtually. She is also the founder of Secret Suppers Worldwide™—an exclusive, one-of-a-kind, supper-style gathering where dynamic business owners connect, have deep conversations, and share ways to be catalysts of change.

www.Moira.ie

DON'T JUST DO–LIVE YOUR WHY

RIDGELY GOLDSBOROUGH

Most people simply DO.
They DO breakfast.
They DO lunch.
They DO dinner.
They DO drinks.
They DO their hair.
They DO laundry.
They DO chores.
They DO their job.
They DO life.
They even DO dumb stuff.
Why?
Who knows . . .
Most people have no idea why they DO what they DO.
They just DO.
Most people hate their jobs.
They don't really know why.
A few like their jobs.
They don't know why either.
Hardly anyone knows why.

- Why do you think the way you think?
- Why do you look the way you look?
- Why do you do what you do?

- Why do you exist?
- Why should we care?

Imagine a world where people actually knew WHY.

When you know WHY, things make more sense. When you know WHY, you gain understanding. Understanding creates clarity. With clarity comes confidence. With confidence, you go after your dreams.

It all starts with WHY. It's time to get reintroduced to yourself. It's time to discover your Mind Type and express your WHY.

Did you realize that every enterprise began with an idea that came from someone? Steve Jobs had an idea. He discussed it with Steve Wosniak. They created Apple. Bill Gates had an idea. He talked to Paul Allen. They created Microsoft. Walt Disney had a vision. Roy Disney backed him up. They birthed Disneyland. The person with the idea is the visionary founder, and the WHY of the business is that person's WHY. The products or services that the business produces become an expression of that WHY.

Consider Apple. Steve Jobs was a rebel who's WHY was to challenge the status quo. As long as the company embraced that WHY, it flourished. Then, in a well-documented power struggle, Steve Jobs was ousted from the company. Apple lost its vision and began a painful downward spiral. Steve Jobs returned in 1997, and by 1998 he cut Apple's product offering from 350 to ten, a dramatic reduction. The company began to challenge the status quo, labeled as "thinking differently." They did so with such radical effectiveness in music distribution that they changed the industry. They did the same thing with mobile devices.

Here's what is so critical to comprehend. Wall Street tells us that Apple is successful because they make great products. They are DEAD WRONG. Apple succeeds because they tell us what they believe, and they attract others who share that belief—loyal, ideal customers that will never switch from their Macs.

Apple users don't care how much they pay. Other computer buyers price-shop.

Apple users don't look for coupons. Other buyers compare features from one manufacturer to another.

Apple users stay up all night to pay full price for the latest product incarnation, even though their current version works perfectly well. Other computer users wait until their old model wears out and then get up on Black Friday looking for a deal.

Apple users identify each other in airports, form part of a fiercely loyal tribe, and debate to the death the superiority of a Mac over a PC.

Apple gets it. They tell us what they believe, NOT what they make or what they do.

If you know your Mind Type and express your WHY clearly, you trigger the reticular activating system of those looking for what you offer.

Your reticular activating system is a group of cells in your brain that filters incoming information. It identifies the information that you deem important. For example, if you search for a parking spot, you see smoke from a tail pipe, brake lights turning red as a car backs out, or a person jingling their keys. If you are not seeking a spot, you drive straight through and see none of those things.

Thousands of people are looking for what you offer right now. Why not make it easy for them to identify you? Your WHY triggers the reticular activating system of those who believe what you believe and seek what you have.

Consider the legal industry, a group of highly intelligent people notoriously horrendous with marketing. Most attorneys tell the world what they know and no more.

John Smith practices family law. His marketing sounds like this:

At the law office of John Smith, we practice family law. We handle divorces, custody cases, paternity issues, alimony and all other areas of family law. We have a professional staff in two convenient locations and offer extensive hours to serve you. Please call us at the number below so that we can help you with your legal needs.

Jane Smith also practices family law. She knows her WHY and expresses it clearly:

At the law office of Jane Smith, we believe in relationships based in trust. Before we work together, we want to get to know you, and we want you to get to know us, so that you feel completely comfortable sharing even the most difficult or intimate details of your case. In that spirit of trust, we can help you get the results you deserve. Please give us a call . . .

John tells you what he does. Jane tells us what she believes.

To slap together cheap divorce papers, John Smith might suffice. However, if you are fearful and have a sensitive divorce situation, John's message will never resonate with you. You want Jane Smith, and when you find her, you instantly know she is the one for you, because she tells you what she stands for.

You don't want everyone. You want those who believe what you believe. These become your ideal clients.

Consider a water company. Normal marketing sounds like this:

At ABC water we have the finest water from the deepest stream with all the vitamins, minerals, and electrolytes you need to fully hydrate your body, especially after *a workout. Want to buy some?*

Contrast this with marketing based on your WHY:

At OUR water, we believe the body is a temple and that only the finest ingredients should ever be put into it. We have the finest water from the deepest stream with all the vitamins, minerals, and electrolytes you need to fully hydrate your body. Want to join the cause?

To change the impact of the message, the company expresses their WHY first and what they offer second. Not everyone will buy OUR water. Bargain hunters will purchase ABC water at the lowest price. OUR water doesn't care. They aren't looking for everyone. They are looking for those that believe that the body is a temple—BECAUSE those customers will never buy ABC water or any water except OUR water, will feel bad about drinking other water, and will seek OUR water everywhere.

What will YOU choose? Will you tell the marketplace what you do? Or will you tell the marketplace what you believe? And you have to do this everywhere.

In business, there is only one piece of real estate under your control—your website. It can't be altered by a new policy, rendered obsolete by an algorithm, made economically unfeasible by fee increases, or taken from you by someone else. It is the single channel over which you have complete command.

Even if other channels generate more activity, on your website you can fully express yourself, showcase your WHY, and let the world know what you stand for. It is also the solitary place where you have command over the user experience. If executed properly, you can grab a visitor, accompany them on a journey, guide them in a direction, and encourage them to take a specific, predetermined action that builds your business.

When someone lands on your site, their next action should be obvious, deliberate, and fully guided by you. Anything that detracts from that experience must be removed. Nothing should remain unless it directs the user to do precisely what you want them to do.

Make sure you answer the following questions: "What am I supposed to do when I land on this website? What action should I take? Is it crystal clear?"

Now that you express your WHY clearly—then what?

Celebrate. The party is just starting!

Picture yourself at the year-end holiday gathering. Your colleagues complain about how hard the year was and how happy they are that it's over. Not you.

Your peers grump about challenging employees and jest about how elated they are to forget them until next year. Not you.

Others bemoan the state of the economy and drown their sorrows with anyone willing to listen. Not you.

You cherish and celebrate your team members. You know their Mind Types and HOW they bring their WHYs to life. They feel energized and inspired, bring their A-game to your business, and are fully invested in your success.

Your message to the marketplace is crystal clear. You attract ideal clients who appreciate your products and services and gladly refer business to you.

As the cookies disappear and the room wishes "good riddance" to the past twelve months, you gaze into the future with complete confidence, knowing that next year will only be better.

Pour yourself another eggnog. You've earned it.

Your WHY is still working.

Ridgely Goldsborough believes in making sense out of things and helping as many people as possible. He founded Mind Types, a revolutionary program to attract ideal clients using brain biology. He has written seventeen books, founded forty-four companies, and created dozens of online programs on success and prosperity.

www.CustomerConversionFormula.com

A SOUL AFFAIR

LORENZO HICKEY

I know there is something I am supposed to do and discover in this magical house. This home and property were calling out to me. All of my dreams were coming true, and all my new wife and I had to do was move in and start the journey of building a new life together in our dream home.

It was a perfect location, next to a mountain full of hiking trails and beautiful views. It was a short six-hour drive to my birth home in San Diego where my beloved family and children were living. I could just jump in my car to go visit whenever I wanted to . . . well, not so fast!

What I was not expecting was that my new mother-in-law moved in with us the weekend we got married. She was a lovely person, kind and good natured, but sadly she was in the early stages of dementia. What transpired over the next four years turned out to be one of the greatest gifts of this lifetime. I call it my soul affair.

The next chapter of this story is that my now-ex-wife (a fantastic lawyer) was married to her job and not generally available for a life with me. To be fair, she tried to make things work, but we were dealing with what I thought (at the time) were extraordinary circumstances. Supporting her mother's needs turned out to be full-time job that ultimately had me home nights and weekends. It was an agreed-upon trade-off for working less in my consulting business while my wife was bringing home the bigger paychecks. This ultimately was the root cause of my soul affair.

I was in a constant personal taffy pull between wanting to be responsible, caring for my mother-in-law, and yet yearning for something more. My dream was real—a million-dollar home, nice cars, opportunities, and a beautiful, smart, kind partner. But my wife was never home and generally not available to me as a partner to spend time with, go to dinners, and be a couple. I had expectations that were not in alignment with hers.

So, with all this time on my hands, I could not avoid that nagging feeling inside that there was something missing in my life. There was a gift in all this, but I couldn't see it, nor did I know how to get started. That's when Joanna came back into my life. She is an amazing intuitive with the best of intentions, and she had been wanting me to work with her for years. In fact, I had previously participated in at least nine months' worth of workshops on various personal development strategies.

It was only after several frustrating years that I made the personal decision to purge my life of things and people that were not necessary. My soul was pushing me to get really clear on who I was and what my intended purpose is for this lifetime.

Back to Joanna, who was the first of some amazing women that transformed my belief systems, connected me to my heart, and to whom I fully and complete gave my soul. At this point, having everything I dreamed of was clearly not enough—my soul was calling for the lessons it needed. So why was Joanna so important to this journey? The short answer is simple: I was living in complete FEAR that I could not leave my marital situation without work and the financial stability I needed. I had given up my personal power to another in exchange for staying at home and caring for my mother-in-law. Not only was I living in fear, but I was generally broke because of several other life-altering challenges.

After ninety days, meeting with Joanna three times a week for forty minutes at a time, during one session she took me on a guided meditation where she created a safe place for me to see my obstacles, gave me clarity on how to address them, and allowed my soul to create enough faith in myself to take some next steps. It was those next steps that led me to Marsha.

Before we go there, two of those gifts I want to share from this transformational journey were revealed. First and foremost, I learned to love myself and who I was. Up to this point in my life, I had never loved me! This was incredibly hard to say for a big, strong athletic guy who grew up as the son of a professional basketball player-turned-alcoholic with his own self-love challenges. Just for the record, my father and I were very much reconciled to our past, and he told me that I was the one who taught him how to love. Go figure!

The second gift was my mother-in-law. As her failing heath required more of my attention, to my surprise, it was my giving and supporting her that felt good to my core. I tried to provide energetic healing (through Reiki) and general playfulness to get her remember her past, and her responsiveness to me was a true gift, one that energized my soul. Before she passed, my name was one of the few she remembered, and I will cherish that fond memory of our times together for the rest of my life.

And then there was Marsha. I joined her group program, only to quit because a group setting was not in the cards for me; I was ready for more personalized attention. That being the case, I did attend the Heart initiation weekend during a full harvest moon in San Diego; it was full of "popcorn miracles" that cleansed and healed my soul. One of the many takeaways after those four days was that I now truly understood and would live into the word *gratitude*.

My soul journey was now in full swing, and I had yet another spirit-guided thought telling me there was someone close to me that would help me. That person turned out to be a psychic named Gina who lived and worked less than a mile from my home. Ultimately, I spent a full year meeting with her and enjoying a multitude of lessons and offerings. The work that struck me most was the introduction to chakra clearing, meeting my spirit guides, and finally closing the doors to my past lives so I could step fully into this life.

What and who could be next? Well, that would be Sabine! Our journey into soul purpose-branding was the final step into a new business called SHAPESHIFT World. Our work put the bow on the idea that you truly have to "shift your thoughts to shape your world." The first step was to take my big vision and turn it into a company brand and strategy that would allow me to do what I love while also allowing for messaging and monetization come into play.

Our client base and business revenues have doubled every year since 2017 when this new company brand was launched. This was not without failures, more challenges, and constant struggles, however. My marriage had ended, I lost my dear mother-in-law, and I ended up living on my own in an apartment after having moved to Arizona for love. Yup . . . at my core I am a lover of love! I wanted to be, live, and enjoy the rest of my life with a person that I believed would make me happy. As it turns out, that was a lie my soul was telling me, and I had believed it completely for over fifty years.

It turns out that the real TRUTH had always been inside my soul, and it was those soul affairs I engaged in that ultimately revealed it to me. I had to LOVE myself first and completely in order for me to heal my heart and soul. It feels so good to put that out to the universe!

The best part has yet to be told. It was yet another woman, Paula, along with Sabine, that brought me to an event where I was to meet my soulmate. This story has yet to be unpacked, but if the past two years are any indication, we are completely on the right track. Why do I say this?

When one initially discovers the true inner meanings of life, they start to reveal the beautiful ways in which we are all connected to one another. We are here to be of service to one another. We are here to support one another in complete collaboration and cooperation. I lock arms with my personal and business partner every day to help and support as many business owners as possible. My soul is destined to create systems and solutions for businesses. I am finally home and loving every day in gratitude, appreciation, and love.

As a serial entrepreneur and recovering accountant, **Lorenzo Hickey** believes these are dynamic times to co-create with a new generation of like-minded individuals moving toward more collaborative and cooperative business models. He is the founder of SHAPESHIFT World, where his wide-ranging experience with small and large businesses assists thousands of clients to succeed.

www.shapeshiftworld.com

DEVELOP A MISTAKE MANAGEMENT PLAN

DOROTHY HUSEN, LMFT

A few months ago, I was sitting at my computer waiting for my course participants to log into our Zoom meeting (the new pandemic version of going onstage). The course I was teaching—*Pain to Possibility: How to Heal at the Emotional Root of Your Chronic Illness, Pain, and Disease*—was the first online seminar I'd ever created—it was my beta course. I was putting together the content for each class as we went, week by week. Now at the halfway point, I was feeling incredibly good about what I'd presented so far and what I'd planned for this session.

As was my practice, thirty minutes prior to the class, I sat down in front of my computer to go over my notes. One last time, I reviewed what I'd decided to teach that day and the way I'd present it. All of a sudden, I got a "better" idea for getting my concepts across and so decided to change my presentation. I began talking through what I'd say in my head. It was such a great idea! I got excited thinking about how impressed my students would be.

My computer binged. Fifteen minutes until my Zoom meeting. I was running out of time to sketch a full outline, let alone seriously practice what I was going to say. *I'll just wing it,* I thought. *You'll be fine; you know this stuff. You've taught it hundreds of times to individual clients.*

As the Zoom alert counted down the minutes in front of me and I hurriedly wrote out a few talking points, the tightness in my stomach (always there before I speak in front of people) began to spread up into my chest and arms and down into my legs. Then, for the first time in years, my body began to shake uncontrollably.

Uh-oh, I thought. *Not again. Not now. Please, not now.* I knew from experience that if these shakes continued, I'd have a real problem on my hands. I also knew that I'd set the stage for this panic attack.

We are all afraid of making mistakes—especially in front of other people. But because of a childhood trauma, my brain is especially prone to reacting to the fear of making a mistake, fear of judgment by others, and fear of the shame all that produces. Before I worked on these issues in therapy, whenever these fears were triggered, my body would go right into the survival response of freeze. And on one occasion, this resulted in my shaking uncontrollably.

I'd been scheduled to lead a seminar for a women's group I belonged to. While waiting to step onto the small platform at the front of the meeting room, a knot in my stomached tightened, my knees started to knock, and then all of me started to shake, including my voice. And I couldn't stop it. Somehow I stumbled through the event. The next day, instead of getting curious about my reaction and looking for its cause, I stuffed my pain and decided I wasn't cut out for leading seminars—or leading anything, for that matter. I vowed never to speak in public again. And for fifteen years following that experience, I didn't speak in public.

In those same fifteen years, however, I did come to terms with my childhood trauma. Healing those wounds through mind/body therapy also healed much of what had made me afraid of speaking in public, that fear of judgment and shame. Eventually I found myself at my local Toastmasters group. My new career as a marriage and family therapist demanded that I speak in public—and now I wanted to; I was ready to.

Baby step-by-baby step, Toastmasters taught me to craft and present a talk, to see criticism as constructive, to recover when I stumbled, and to find my voice and self-confidence. Still, when I was waiting to make my first full speech in front of my Toastmasters group, I felt that knot in my stomach again, and I feared I'd start to shake. Miraculously I didn't. With one full breath, the knot untied itself. I became calm, walked into my Toastmasters meeting, and gave my speech without freezing. Then I declared myself "cured" of the shakes.

That was a mistake that wouldn't reveal itself until the day, five years later, when I found myself sitting in front of my computer, staring at my Zoom alert, and shaking uncontrollably once again. Though I employed the self-soothing techniques I'd learned in therapy (deep breathing, con-necting to my traumatized inner child), I was too far into the attack to turn it around. So I got up from my computer, drank a glass of water, and went outside for a walk. Thankfully, I made it back to the com-puter in time and was able to control my body long enough to teach my class—though I shook slightly for the entire hour. Afterward, it took me four hours to recover sufficiently enough to move on with my day.

The mistake I made that day was setting myself up to likely make more mistakes in front of people—a trigger I mistakenly thought was in my past. That's a lot of mistakes for one morning.

When we are faced with a mistake (or several), we have a choice. We can beat ourselves up, which typically keeps our triggers hot and compounds any negative fallout. We can stuff it and let the shame of it limit our lives (as I had done with my first public speaking experience). Or we can accept that mistakes are a part of living fully and use ours as opportunities to learn and grow.

By this time in my life, I'd had enough therapy to be able to see my mistakes as opportunities. Once I calmed down from this one, I thought carefully about what had happened. I started by acknowledging that even though I was more emotionally healthy than I was twenty years ago, I was (and am) obviously still capable of being triggered—especially when doing something new in front of people. I also realized that my desire to impress my students only put more pressure on that trigger. Finally, it occurred to me that the reason I'd avoided triggering the shakes at that first Toastmasters speech and for the dozens of public speaking events I've done since was because I'd prepared for those events and stuck to my plan.

All good things for me to be aware of. So good, in fact, that I developed a Mistake Management Plan—Accept, Prepare, Recover, Reflect—so I could put what I'd learned from this mistake into use whenever I'm speaking in public:

- *Accept.* As soon as I feel the fear of judgment coming on, I remind myself that mistakes are going to happen. They're to be expected and so accepted. When I bring this kind of awareness to a situa-tion, I take back my agency from any triggers.
- *Prepare.* I now acknowledge that "winging it" isn't the best plan for me. I'm not cured. My healing is ongoing, and mistakes can be

triggers. It's best to avoid mistakes where I can by preparing and practicing before speaking in front of people. Changing my mind at the last minute doesn't serve me.

- *Recover.* When I do make a mistake and get triggered, I remind myself that I have a plan for recovery, and then I execute that plan. I take a deep breath to reconnect to my body and then to my true self. I go inward and talk nonjudgmentally to myself. I tell myself that I'm good enough just the way I am, and I don't need to chase admiration from other people. I remind myself that I do what I do to help people, the way I've been helped. I don't do it to impress them. (In fact, I now write this at the top of every lesson plan.)
- *Reflect.* Once my head is clear and my body calm, I take time to think about the mistake. I learn what I can from it. And then I let it go, along with any negative emotions it created for me.

The only real mistake we can make as speakers is to not be mentally prepared for the inevitable mistakes we're going to make. Nobody wants to mess up, but we also don't want to be so afraid of mistakes that fear limits us. Whether we lose our train of thought, have technical difficulties, or start to shake while on stage (or on Zoom), we want to accept our mistakes, learn from them, and count each as a treasured reminder that we're not stagnant but growing with every experience.

Dorothy Husen, LMFT, is a mind-body coach, speaker, and author. She specializes in working with people suffering from chronic pain due to childhood trauma, abuse, or ongoing stress. Her book, *Breaking the Chains of Transgenerational Trauma: My Journey from Surviving to Thriving,* is available on her website.

www.dorothyhusen.com

TAKE A DEEP BREATH AND STEP INTO YOUR VISION

KRISTINA JENSEN

Thanks to speaking, I get be my own boss at 2:47 p.m. in Erie, Pennsylvania, on a Tuesday afternoon. My laptop is open on my desk (i.e., kitchen island), I'm listening to the Bach's *Brandenburg Concertos*, and natural light is streaming in behind me through gorgeous stained glass as I write. It feels like I have been preparing to write this chapter for three years now. That's how long I have been coaching online, and my business finally has taken off through speaking. Four weeks ago I led "The Faith in Business Summit: How to Hear God's Voice in Difficult Times So That You Pivot Instead of Panic." That changed everything for me.

I chose this theme because I am a pastor who also has an online business as a faith coach. I specialize in helping people find congruence in their faith and business. I wanted to hear what entrepreneurs who led with faith had to say about hearing God's voice in the pivotal moments of their lives. Were there common patterns about how God spoke to people or the lessons that people had to learn before their businesses took a turn into the black? What surprising things did people learn about God and about themselves along the way? What advice did they have for people starting out and for those already on the path? What was their advice for people in transition and those just getting off the ground? What services and/or nuts-and-bolts help could they offer people to make the way that much smoother? The answers to these questions became the content of the interviews.

Over the course of six weeks, I pulled together a summit with forty-four speakers. We registered about 650 participants. My email list grew from nineteen people to 580 (after people dropped off once the summit was over), and my Facebook group grew from 110 to over 350. Within the first three days of the summit, people attending told me that the interviews were life-changing, and by the following week, I had sold three spots in my twelve-spot mastermind. Making the decision to leave my part-time pastor position became a reality—and this was a good thing because things were becoming toxic. My husband, also a pastor, lost his job due to church infighting, and we knew we had to find a new place to live. We were able to take the leap of faith to move to a new community we love rather than stay in a situation where life would be stable but leave us always wanting for more.

I submitted my resignation and started on a new adventure of full-time entrepreneurship. Is it scary? Sure! However, thanks to the increase of my audience size from the virtual "stage" of this summit and future stages to come, I know that as long as I continue to show up, there will always be work for me to do. For that, I will always be grateful.

Speaking has taught me we always have the choice—staring at us front and center—to *take action*. All we have to do is get up the courage to keep taking bold steps forward. It doesn't matter what we are going through, whether it's a little or a lot; what matters is that we take a deep breath and let our vision guide us rather than our fear. The important piece is that we take much **bolder** steps than we feel we are ready for. Why? Because of the lesson this stage taught me, that I now share with you: ***Our lives will change in proportion to the change we are willing to make.***

Let me share with you a pivotal moment from this experience that you can start using right away. Change asking IF something can or should or will get done to HOW it can or should or will get done—and just GO FOR IT. At first, I wasn't sure if I should do the summit at all. My husband was about to lose his job, and because he is a pastor, that would mean that we would have to move. I didn't know whether I should focus on getting my family settled in a new location or revving up my online business.

I reached out to friends and mentors, prayed, and read Scripture as I discerned what to do. My coaches were instrumental in helping me to see that God never leads us through difficult situations by calling us to quit—God leads us by walking through the fire with us and allowing us to breathe even as the waves are crashing our boat into the rocky shore. I decided to go for it. I had no idea at the time where we would soon be living, how we would pay the rent, or what my husband's job situation and my business would look like.

Throughout each interview during the summit, not only did I provide each speaker a chance to showcase their work to an expanded audience, but God also molded and shaped me as well as each individual participant who joined the summit. As people saw the hope that I received for my own life, they saw God at work in their own. God showed me that GOOD things were planned for my life, for my family, and for my work in the world through my business. The waters got rough, and I realized that God was asking ME to take the helm of the ship and steer it through the storm rather than throwing my decision to fate. God was asking me to stand up for myself and use all my gifts and talents to make a difference in this world—immediately.

Speaking is so powerful because it is a medium that gives you the ability to connect directly through story, insight, wonder, and emotion in a way that marks both the speaker and each person present forever. Speaking reminds each of us that we have an impact on this earth—that we matter—that our voice IS sacred.

Friend, if you are reading this, it is because you have both a passion and a calling. I may be a pastor, but I am not the only one who has been "ordained" by God. *Ordination* is simply a fancy word that means "set apart by God." Friend, **YOU** have been set apart by God for a purpose. **How** do you plan on using your voice—your sacred voice—to speak that purpose into being? What is the first bold step you are going to take? You've got this! And remember, God's got **YOU**.

I'll be praying for you and your future as you read this. I know that first step can be a doozy—and really, who are we fooling? The second and the third step can feel just like the first! But let me tell you, friend, your very own U-Haul is ready and waiting just outside your door, all your belongings piled up and ready for your new destination. It's called the stage . . .

Where are you going? Are you seeking a new career? What do you envision? More freedom with your time? Your money? Your kids?

Wherever you are going and whatever your vision, I'm here to tell you—the stage is the fastest vehicle to get you there! All you have to do is take it one step at a time . . .

For over fifteen years as an ordained pastor, **Kristina Jensen** has helped hundreds of people rebuild their relationship with faith. She now loves helping entrepreneurs and professionals find congruence throughout their faith, life, and business. Kristina enjoys cooking with her kids, singing, walks with the family dog, and watching movies.

www.kristinaleejensen.com

"HOW ABOUT THAT FAKE SMILE!"

LATASHA "LT" JIMERSON

"Happy Monday, Mrs. Jimerson; this is my brother, Joseph. His first period class is right next door. Can he sit in your class with me until his teacher gets here?"

"This is my favorite class."

"Oh my gosh, Mrs. Jimerson, like, how do you know everything about my life?"

"You are my favorite teacher."

"Mrs. Jimerson, you are a real teacher."

"Mrs. Jimerson, can I call you Miss Jay?"

"Oh, my gosh, Mrs. Jimerson, you sound just like my mom."

"No, way, you act just like my auntie."

"I bet you cuss a lot at home, huh, Mrs. Jimerson?"

"You know you turn into that angry Black Mom when you are home with your kids, huh, Mrs. Jimerson?"

"Can I just stay here in this room with you all day?"

These are words uttered by various teenagers with whom I have worked with over the past seventeen years as a classroom teacher.

I started teaching in my twenties, and I absolutely loved it—at first. I loved working with parents, students, and even some of the curriculum. My passion was helping teenagers learn new things. I yearned to witness the "light bulb moment" when they finally understood something that I had explained eighty-seven times. I loved being able to help children search and find the "light bulb" buried inside their scattered brains.

My teaching days were highlighted by me greeting my students at the door. I played a game with myself to see how long it took me to help my students "turn their frowns upside down." Seriously, this was a fun game to me. I would crack jokes and poke fun of them at the door before they entered in an attempt to lighten the mood immediately.

In addition to cracking jokes, I also complimented my students on their hairdos, outfits, punctuality, or work ethic. I always found something positive to say to each and every child that walked through my door. History classes might be dry and boring in other places, but not in my classroom.

Having the ability to brighten my students' day with my smile was a gift. I learned that a smile is a special gift from God. Not because I think I am so great, but because of what other people say to me about my smile. They say my smile brings warmth and coziness into the room. Many have said that my smile brings joy to their hearts. This situation is so interesting and ironic to me.

Although my smile has brought joy to hundreds of students and their families, it has served as a mask for me. It was a mask that covered up my true feelings about what was going on in my personal life. The truth behind my "fake smile" was that for over five years, I was deeply depressed, fearful, and lonely. The stress of having a career, raising a family, and holding together a marriage was breaking me down. I was overwhelmed and afraid to ask for help. I knew I was in trouble, but I felt I had nowhere to go.

Every day I would write my feelings in my journal and pray that the bad emotions would go away. Every night I cried myself to sleep because I felt so lonely. Every month, I would go get a massage and a pedicure, hoping that would make me feel better. Every June I would update my resume and prepare to find a less stressful job.

But every time I made up my mind to finally quit my job, I would hear the voices of my students saying how much they loved me. I would envision their love notes taped to my computer screen or stapled on the wall near my desk. The best notes came from the troubled child who was transferred into my class because no other teacher could handle him or her, or the "at-risk" kid who wore baggy pants and sat in the back row with his head down. Those are the kids that I could reach and teach.

Today I am no longer a classroom teacher. I have decided to teach and reach others on a larger scale. Today I am an author, speaker, and book coach. My *Monday Motivational* videos live on YouTube and on the cell phones of one hundred of my closest friends and family members. I started creating motivational talks three years ago to encourage myself. The videos cheered me up, so I decided to share them with other people. The more I shared them, the more other people started sharing them too. Although I no longer make videos, I still love watching them. It is pretty cool that I can encourage myself.

Another passion of mine is coaching. I am now coaching adults who want to learn to write books that heal people. My clients are retired professionals who are legacy-driven. They love my coaching sessions because I teach them twenty-first-century skills such as word-processing, editing, formatting, revising, proofreading, and self-publishing. Lately my coaching business has been attracting administrators, teachers, and writers. We talk about their life stories and the pivotal events in their lives.

Together, we laugh, we cry, and we create, craft, polish, and publish books that heal people. This is my NEW job, and I love it. This is the job that I created for myself. I am still teaching, but now I am not limited by the four walls of a classroom. I work from home or wherever I want.

My life is amazing.

My life has not always been amazing, though.

I was born in Newark, Jersey, in 1976 to a teenage mother. She walked across the stage with me at her high school graduation. She was eighteen, and I was two. By the time she was twenty-one, she had three kids. Immediately after high school, she got married and moved us to North Carolina and then California in the early 1980s.

My sister and brother never knew their dad the way I did. I heard screams at night when he was beating my mom. She would come into our room at night, move our bunk bed to block the door, and go to sleep with us kids. This went on for years. I was her protector and confidant because her husband did not bother me. He was intimidated by me because I was not his child. The thought of me telling my father was enough for him to back off.

When my mom decided to leave my stepfather, we instantly became homeless. Everyday living became a nightmare. We moved in and out of friends' houses and battered women's shelters. My siblings and I learned how to make friends quickly because we were always moving. We had to be secretive, though, because we were on the run from my stepfather. If he caught us, he made us go home with him, and the beatings picked up again. When my mom was at work, we were left with babysitters. Some of them watched us, some of them ignored us, and some of them abused us. We were treated like trash. This period of my life was so traumatizing that I do not even remember most of it. I literally buried much of it deep down into my psyche, hoping that it would never surface.

However, the memories do come up at the worst possible times. They come up and interrupt my life when I am just trying to be happy. All I want to do is smile and pray that everything will be okay. Most days, that is so; other days, not so much. Today I look at my life and learn the lessons God wants me to learn. I do not question anything; I just move forward.

As a wife, I encourage women to trust God as the head and protector of marriage. As a mom, I tell my daughters to pursue their dreams without hesitation. As a human being, I tell people to fake it until you make it—and smile. I encourage you to smile for three reasons: one because it is one activity that you control 100 percent; two, it is free; and three because it is contagious! Keep smiling, even if you feel like a fake, and have faith that one day your smile will become real.

Latasha "LT" Jimerson is an author, book coach, course creator, and speaker. Her online school currently offers seventeen courses that teach personal development. Latasha's expertise is coaching writers to become authors. To watch her educational webinars on self-publishing and gain access to FREE e-books, visit her website.

http://www.myfirstbook.org/

HOW YOUR BRAND "SPEAKS" CREATES YOUR IMPACT

RICH KOZAK

Y ou are ready. You are determined. You *know* that your business, your work, or your gift can impact others' lives in a positive way. Right now you are feeling called, compelled, maybe even driven, to take what you do to a higher level. You're ready to give it an identity, to brand it, to make it really come alive and thrive! You want it to touch a lot of lives. You want your work to make a significant impact. You want to touch the world. But you are wondering and struggling with "How do I do THAT?"

Imagine yourself talking directly one-on-one with a deeply experienced professional who has decades of expertise in defining and languaging an individual's most powerful umbrella brand: an impact-driven brand that perfectly represents the uncopiable uniqueness of the individual behind the brand. I hope I have your attention. I am writing this chapter specifically for **you** to reframe your understanding and to give you clarity. I know that you have been created with unique gifts, talents, and purpose, and that your life journey adds to that unique portfolio of "you." The result: your defined and languaged *desired brand* is completely congruent with the impact you want your thriving brand to make on others. It's also completely congruent with your heart.

As a deep-listening, heart-connecting branding expert, which "golden nugget" am I going share with you? Which guideline will propel your freshly defined and languaged brand to faster success and impact, to come alive and attract like a magnet? What do I tell you right now that most brands small or large simply don't know, or truly don't understand or act upon?

> The Clarity With Which
> Your Brand Speaks
> Shapes Its Impact.
> —Rich Kozak, *RichBrands*

To ensure that this nugget lands and stays with you, let's unwrap its three key words—*Clarity, Speaks,* and *Impact.* Before we unwrap them, we'll define the word *Brand* so you clearly understand it and so its "buzz word" nature does not frustrate you or add to your struggle.

Simply put, a *Brand* is a perception. It's the perception someone has of you. It is *not* the perception you have of yourself. It is how people see you, how you come across, how you show up, what they give you credit for, or what they give you *no credit* for. Everything you and your Brand says and does creates that perception.

We feel comfortable with a person who shows consistent behavior because we know what to expect from him or her. Likewise, consistent language and behavior and expectations from a Brand make us feel comfortable with that Brand. The inverse is also true: Inconsistent language and behavior create discomfort and confusion, misinformation, *no credit,* and inaction—and this makes brands fall flat.

Impact

Like a car crash's impact causes significant permanent change, the impact a brand makes on a person causes significant permanent change. There are different levels of impact. For example: understanding; reframing how a person sees themselves or their world; developing new habits; teaching; contributing to community. Note that a defined Brand's desired impacts are written as intentional decisions made in advance selecting specific types of individuals or groups as the target audiences of the Brand. An impact-driven Brand includes written *impact statements* that specify the highest value impact you can clearly see in your mind's eye that your brand will have on a specific type of individual or group.

Speaks

This must include clear word pictures the Brand paints of what you see in the future for the people whose lives you will impact.

The Brand must "speak" nonverbally with its consistent identifiable brand imagery, design, color palate, logo, and tagline.

And to *come alive*, the Brand must "speak" *consistent language that transfers energy*. It begins with the first impression when the Brand "says what it does" and continues consistently. Its special words and phrases are unique to the Brand, acting as "intangible Brand promises," attracting the Brand's target audiences, and setting expectations for what they will receive when they allow the Brand to touch their life. For example:

A broadly skilled financial planner for individuals, families, and businesses now serves as the founder and CEO of a Brand named MONEY TRUTH & LIFE, which "Provides Written Wisdom That Strengthens Families for Abundant Living" and serves as "The Voice of Money Truth." This brand has become the voice of facts and expert guidance without any self-serving agenda that so many people need in today's world.

An experienced Information Technology (IT) managed services provider whose caring concern about increasing frequency and gravity of internet criminal threats to the smallest US businesses and the livelihood of millions of families focuses his Brand and its promise this way: "COMPLIANCE SPECIALISTS: Protecting You to Grow" and specializes in "True Small Business Data Security™."

A coach and certified trainer of Neuro Linguistic Programming (NLP) who wants to serve first by guiding ex-addicts to a positive future and then by improving their success in business and relationships launched her Brand as "EMPOWERING GROWTH." Her tagline evolves from "Renewing Your Life After Addiction" to "Freeing You to Transform Your Life."

When your Brand "speaks" from a live or virtual stage, you have a great opportunity to shape the emotional dynamics of the audience's response to your message, much like a good orchestra conductor manages the dynamics of a symphony.

Clarity

It is in unwrapping Clarity that we get to the heart of the Brand. When clarity is missing, its lack prevents a Brand from magnetically attracting those whom the Brand most wants to impact. Two common examples of missing clarity are 1) a Brand's envisioned impacts might be undefined, and 2) its impact statements are vague or lack specificity. A Brand might "speak" using inconsistent language that doesn't transfer energy, whether on its website, to its prospects, or from a real or virtual stage. Like a finely cut gem, a brand's clarity comprises many facets, including its:

- purpose, vision, expectations, worldview, desired outcomes, and what it seeks for others
- envisioned possibilities
- clarity of understanding target audiences' care-abouts, what blocks them or holds them back
- heart and care for those it envisions impacting
- clarity about the impacts it envisions making
- clarity of language as it "speaks" so that its target audiences truly hear
- clarity about the characteristics and categories of expertise for which the Brand must become known to make its envisioned impacts
- clarity of language in its prewritten testimonials and endorsements for its target audiences that helps to ensure it to makes its impacts

If you sense that defining your Brand's clarity is an academic exercise, please consider this lesson I learned at seven years old from my passionate, fun violin teacher, Carmen Cavuto. In his special way of demonstrating the violin's versatility and beautiful possibilities, he chose a simple tune (think "Joy to the World" or "The Itsy Bitsy Spider"). First Mr. Cavuto simply played the notes on the page and stopped. Then he closed his eyes and played the exact same notes while allowing his heart to add dynamics, breath, pace, pause, and flourish. What he found in his heart turned those notes into music. That moment's impact on me was permanent and deep. It's lesson has lasted a lifetime.

I recommend you apply that lesson to defining and languaging your most powerful umbrella Brand—an *impact-driven Brand* that perfectly represents you. Close your eyes, literally or figuratively, and picture what your Brand is doing when it thrives. Then envision those individuals on whom you clearly see in your mind's eye making a high-value impact.

Writing these down, you feel yourself resonating with them. These are the impacts your heart really wants to make. The three, or seven, or twelve that you clearly envision and write down will not be your only impacts, but they will serve to define The Brand YOU Will Become. In fact, they will serve to define the Brand You MUST Become to make the impacts you envision. The process is step-by-step, and its results are guaranteed by design.

The clarity with which your brand speaks shapes its impact.

The three most important missing pieces in most Brands are 1) clarity in how it paints the future it sees for its target audiences, 2) clarity of the highest value impacts it envisions making on its target audiences, and 3) consistent language that transfers energy.

When that clarity and consistent language is in place, as a result everything your Brand says and does now creates a consistent perception, a consistent Brand. Now what your Brand "speaks" is totally aligned with your desired impacts. Your Brand begins attracting exactly what it needs to achieve those impacts, because of the clarity with which your Brand speaks.

Rich Kozak founded *RichBrands* as rocket fuel for individuals who want their brand to impact others' lives. Rich is the sage voice of IMPACT-Driven Branding. This passionate speaker, author, trainer, and coach focuses his deep-listening style and decades of experience on ensuring that your personal business brand comes alive and speeds your impact.

www.RichBrands.org

THE POWER OF OUTSOURCING

ANNE LACKEY

few months ago, I was having dinner with my aunt and uncle, and they shared a compelling story with me about my Grandmother Mamie. As with a lot of our grandparents in my generation, Grandmother Mamie had a hard life. From being born during the Depression to several wars, she learned to make do, adapt, and innovate.

Being the parents of three children, my grandparents lived in an efficient three-bedroom, one-bath home that completely served their needs. Can you imagine sharing a bath with your kids in today's world? No thank you. And yet back then it was perfectly acceptable.

They had air-conditioning in their bedroom through a window unit. I remember that on hot summer days, I would sneak into their room to cool off. I never thought anything about it growing up. But that small room with the air-conditioning was a multipurpose room. It was where my grandmother worked and helped to support her family.

You see, I never knew that my grandmother worked from home for an insurance company. She would assess fire damage, write up the reports, and submit them to the office. She was a top producer in the company, working at home with three kids. She was an original remote team member when there was minimal technology. She had a desk and a landline and a small air-conditioned room.

How was she a top producer? She learned to outsource. It turns out my grandmother couldn't type. She was determined not to let that stop her, so she hired a typist. She would do the forms and analysis and then submit them to the typist. She was able to do twice as much. She focused on what she was good at and had others do what she wasn't. This enabled her to be the top producer.

Often in our lives, we hold on to tasks that we don't enjoy because of three things: fear of losing control, not enough time to train, or lack of knowledge. Each of these things keeps us from our Zone of Genius, as Gay Hendrick calls it in her book *The Big Leap*. (If you haven't read it, I highly recommend it.)

Fear of losing control is probably the hardest thing I help CEOs work on. You see, you can never scale if you don't let go. If you put in the right documentation, hire well, and trust your team, you will be happier, have more clients, make more money, and have more impact in the world.

Not enough time to train is a fallacy. It is an excuse to stay small. We all make time for the things that are important to us. If you are serious about growing your business and having a huge impact in the world, you will have to teach others to do those tasks you no longer want or need to do.

Lack of knowledge is 100 percent fixable. You can learn to do anything you set your mind to do. The question becomes whether you should hire a professional or learn to do it yourself.

I will share a personal example with you. I came out of corporate from the IT and HR sector. I love technology and have always been an early adopter. When my husband and I started our first couple of businesses, I was the company's IT department. Anything I didn't know how to fix, I would spend hours researching in order to solve it. A few years ago, we were having some more complex IT issues. On the way to dinner with my husband, he turned to me and said, "You're fired!"

"What do you mean, 'I'm fired'?" I replied.

"You can no longer support the IT needs of our company. We need you focused on other things."

He then proceeded to call my old boss and ask him to put together a service contract for us since we needed to get our IT in order and I could no longer do it.

After the initial shock wore off, I found it to be quite liberating. No longer was I needed to work on these computer issues. Now, whenever anyone complains, I politely say, "Call Eclipse. They can fix it." While I could do it, it really wasn't the best use of my time, energy, and effort. I could spend hours researching and learning to keep up with all the changes, but in the end, it was much better for our business to hire a professional who specialized in this.

Another big stumbling block with CEOs getting the help needed is not knowing the options for finding help. I have found there are three types of assistance that can help a CEO accomplish their big dreams: the freelancer, the call center/outsourcer, and the employee/virtual employee.

The freelancer is a great resource for projects. They can do things like create a logo, craft a marketing piece, provide copy for a sequence, and so on. These people generally focus on a specific skill, work for many clients, and are paid by the job.

The call center/outsourcer is great for ongoing tasks such as receptionist services, sales appointments, lead generation, or other skilled work. Outsourcers are shared services for a common goal, and you typically purchase a block of hours or a pay a flat fee plus usage for the use of their time and skills. The advantage is that you can begin getting the help you need without the commitment of hiring a full-time person.

The employee/virtual employee is a person who works exclusively for you. They work the hours you set, work on your software platforms under your direction, and are managed by you. This allows you to have more control over the training and results. An added benefit of using virtual employees is that you can save money by hiring outside of the US, saving anywhere from 50 to 75 percent over local hires.

As business owners, we don't have to know everything. We just need to look at the things we are good at and enjoy doing and then hire others—whether on a contract basis as I do with my IT services or as an employee/virtual employee—to do those things for us.

It's funny to me that five years after starting HireSmart, I first heard my grandmother's story. You see, HireSmart is all about helping our clients do more of what they are fantastic at while letting our virtual employees be the most productive and best in the business.

If you have ever considered a virtual employee, let's chat.

Anne Lackey is the co-founder of HireSmart Virtual Employees. In the past two decades, she has started seven successful businesses. A three-time bestselling author, recruiter, trainer, and consultant, she helps business owners to scale and grow through the power of leveraging other people's time and talents.

www.meetwithanne.com

A NEW CHAPTER IN MY LIFE

CATHERINE M. LAUB, ACM

This holiday season begins a new chapter in my life. I am selling my house and moving from Long Island, New York, to Pennsylvania. I am taking this journey alone and am looking forward to it.

My husband, Tony, died February 25, 2020, and I am alone for the first time in my life at age sixty-two.

I tried to stay in our house, but I soon realized the cost to live in New York was too much for me. My only income has been social security disability. For seven years I have tried to create a profitable business, but I ended up spending 90 percent more than I earned. For now, my business efforts have been put on hold.

Tony and I were already searching for a new home in the Poconos before he got sick. I continued the search after he died, and after only two days I found my ideal home in a fifty-five-plus community. I do not know anyone in Pennsylvania, but I am excited because I will meet new people, and I love making friends.

I am looking forward to decorating my new home with my Christmas villages and wonderful ornaments. Next year I will advertise to decorate other people's homes for the holidays. I love celebrating the holidays, beginning in November. It's the highlight of my year, especially because I get to spend more time with my kids and grandchildren. This year will be different, but I will enjoy the season wherever I am.

My ideal holiday plan this year was to stay in a B&B where they have decorating, baking, singing, and so on like on the Hallmark Channel's Christmas shows. Unfortunately, because of COVID there will not be any celebrations like that. So I will plan it for next year. Tony did not like the holidays because he found them stressful. Now that I am alone, I plan to make the most of them.

I usually bake cookies with my family, but this year I will do so alone after I move. I'll use my grandmother's recipe for *Pfeffernüsse* cookies, which is quite different than the store-bought ones. I roll the dough and use cookie cutters. I also make other varieties: sugar cookies, chocolate chip balls, green and red M&M cookies, and peanut butter cookies.

Once the new year comes, I will venture out and meet new people and pray for things to get better so we can gather in groups. My parents and I used to attend bingo weekly when they were alive. It is not the same without them! Bingo is my favorite pastime, so I'm planning to go often once the pandemic is over.

My business consists of psychic readings, a podcast, and speaking about mental illness through my own journey.

For years I struggled with suicidal thoughts and was hospitalized many times. When the thoughts became severe, I made sure to get to the hospital, where the doctors would adjust my medications and I could rest from the stress that caused the thoughts.

Since Tony died, I have not been depressed, and I have no more suicidal thoughts. Unfortunately, I now realize that a lot of the negativity I experienced came from our relationship. We loved each other deeply, but we also fought a lot. What I did not realize was that Tony was depressed due to financial stress. He never discussed it with me, and I did not know the extent of the problems until he became ill with cancer last year. Spiritually, I am an empath (I absorb other people's negative energies), so I absorbed Tony's depression, and with my own mental illnesses, I became incessantly depressed.

Tony stayed home until the night before he died. I was not there mentally during his last days. Our house was constantly full of people, and the negativity caused me much heartache and stress. My new anxiety medication caused havoc, and I was told that I did many things I do not remember. I passed out a couple times, was told that I got very nasty with everyone, was very suicidal, and on Tony's last night home, I was hallucinating terribly. Because I am an empath, I never thought to protect myself against all that negative energy.

Tony was brought by ambulance to a hospice facility where he died the next morning. I thought I had enough time to be with him, so another ambulance brought me to the hospital. I needed to find out what was wrong with me. We did not realize it was the medication until after Tony was gone. I stopped taking it and was fine.

I am grateful that I do remember talking with him before he left. He told me something was wrong, and I said, "Yes, it's time. You fought a great battle, but it's over." A policeman was there because of the way I had been acting, and he took me away from Tony. That was the last time I saw him alive. I miss him terribly and still cry myself to sleep. I allow myself to cry because it cleanses the soul, and I know it will eventually stop with better days to come.

God gave me a mission to speak about my journey to support others in their journeys of stress and mental illness. I recognize that to be there for others who struggle, I needed to go through much heartache myself.

My slogan is "Brighten Your Day with Turquoise." Turquoise is a soothing color and incredibly supportive for one's mood. It creates emotional balance and stability. I wear turquoise clothes and headbands when I attend my networking events and business gatherings. This keeps me calm and gives me confidence when I am speaking with others. I used to be extremely nervous when I gathered with others in any setting—even my own wedding. Once I learned about turquoise, it took most of that nervousness away.

I know Tony is watching over me, and I want to make him proud of me. My continuous illnesses often kept me from moving forward. I had several surgeries, and twice I had Broken Heart Syndrome (Takosubo Cardiomyopathy) due to the stress of losing my mother, Tony becoming ill, and then ultimately losing him. Along the way there have been many hospitalizations for suicidal thoughts and attempts.

Now I am moving forward in the right direction. My name will be known by many as "The Turquoise Lady," and I will be thrilled that I am helping so many people feel better.

I love people and want to inspire as many as I can with my many stories. My podcast will begin again in the new year, and I plan to interview people who help others through various modalities. I have done some great interviews over the past few years, and I am looking forward to doing many more.

Another dream of mine is to host quarterly summits with interviews and speeches from therapists, doctors, and people who also struggle with mental illness. With COVID, many people have become overly stressed and need support coping, so I think this would be very beneficial.

My cardiologist has told me it is time for me to get into a routine of walking at least half an hour a day. I have fat around my heart, and he is concerned because I already have coronary artery disease. This does not worry me. I have confidence that I will begin walking in my new neighborhood and the weight and fat around my heart will dissolve. God would not bring me this far to help others and let me continue with ill health.

I will continue writing, which I love. So far, I have contributed to twenty books and have written one of my own. I enjoy writing and am proud of my accomplishments. I know the future will be great, and there will be travel and collaborations with many people. I know that sharing my journey will inspire others to persevere in their own challenges, and together we will rise to new heights!

Recently widowed, **Catherine M. Laub, ACM,** hosts her self-produced podcast *The Celestial Spoon*, is an award-winning inspirational author, speaker, psychic/medium, spiritual guide, and advocate for mental illness. She guides people to understand they can live with illness and still have a happy life.

www.catherinemlaub.com

SHINE A LIGHT

NATALIE LAVELOCK, RN-MSN

According to the *Oxford English Dictionary*, *visibility* is commonly defined as "the state of being able to see or be seen, or the degree to which something has attracted general attention; prominence."

To be seen—it's the thing we strive for as entrepreneurs, right? Why else would we spend countless hours on social media, our own little personal stage designed for the world to be able to see us at any moment. We love to see those "views" and "likes" and comments popping up on our posts. It's also why we will pay good money to get a spot on someone else's stage. Someone who has a bigger name, a larger following . . . more "visibility."

I laugh to myself as I write this at the irony of someone who spends their life helping others expand their visibility hiding in the background and writing a chapter in a book about visibility. You see, I'm the one you come to when you need a scalable coaching program, training program, or product (i.e., online course, home study kit, etc.)—the thing that is going to help your business reach more people, make more money, and have an even greater impact. But my role in that is to partner with you from behind the scenes. I make sure the learning process is in place so that your clients get results—consistently—and that your business model is both sustainable and scalable. I am NOT the attention grabber; I do NOT seek to be centerstage myself. Yet here I am.

That being said, you can imagine my surprise when I had planned to sponsor an event and—only a week beforehand—found out that I had won a "special prize": a spotlight speaking spot onstage . . . in front of two hundred-plus people!

As my ears took in that information and my brain tried to process it, every insecurity in my body showed up at once. "Who am I to be on stage? No one cares what I have to say. What *am* I going to say? Can I give this 'gift' to someone else so I don't have to do it? OMGoodness, what is going on?"

The funny thing is, I'm used to speaking in front of groups of people. I have taught college courses and spoken at statewide conferences. I trained doctors and nurses for years as the hospital's Clinical Nurse Educator. It was my job to make sure they had the information, education, and training they needed to not only care for patients at the bedside, but to be at the top of their game when seconds count and things go wrong. But in my mind, all of that was different. That was EDUCATIONAL, not INSPIRATIONAL. And it definitely was not the type of motivational speaking needed to get a crowd of people to leave their cozy seats to rush to the back of the room in order to buy something from me!

In the days leading up to the event, I bet I wrote and rewrote my "speech" thirty times! And with each new draft, I got more and more nervous, more and more anxious. I prayed that I wouldn't forget what to say and look like a complete idiot!

Fast-forward to the minutes before I was to go onstage. As I waited in the nearly empty hallway to be called into the green room to get mic'd up, I was pacing and pacing, going over and over and over my speech in my head. Someone walked up to me and said, "Hey, are you getting ready to speak?" When I said yes, he said, "Would you like a couple pointers?" I laughed and said, "Sure," while what I was really thinking was, *Buddy, I'm ten minutes from walking out on that stage, and I have absolutely no clue what I'm doing. Pointers would have been helpful a week ago—I just want to survive this and not look like a complete idiot!*

Little did I know that this guy was not just some nice person taking pity on this walking disaster—he was a veteran speaker and a master speaker trainer! I tried to listen to what he was saying, believing that ANY help at that point would be worthwhile, while my entire body was caught somewhere between convulsively shaking with nerves, wanting to throw up, and trying to decide if there was still time to escape.

He told me that when I got onstage, I should plant my feet and NOT move! There was to be no pacing like a caged animal! Then he basically rewrote my entire speech TEN MINUTES BEFORE I WALKED ONSTAGE! Oddly enough, while I would have expected that to totally derail me and make the situation even worse, something about his demeanor actually helped ground me a little. Now don't get me wrong, I was still on board the "hot-mess-express," but I had just the tiniest bit more confidence, and I felt just the tiniest bit more settled. And it was enough.

I took what he said, went onstage, planted my feet in one place, and delivered my first ever "sell from the stage speech." And guess what? I got clients from that event, and it changed the trajectory of my business and my life!

I realized in that moment that when you choose to become visible, you have the opportunity to change someone's life! It doesn't matter whether it's visible on a stage, social media, or just seeing someone in need and making the decision to step out of the shadows in that moment to offer help. Your visibility can be someone's lifeline. Yes, it's easy to get caught up in chasing status, money, and influence. Being onstage, commanding the attention of an entire room of people, can be very seductive if you're not careful. But that's not what it's all about for me.

In the years that have passed since that first speaking engagement, being onstage has become less and less about me—about how I look or whether I goof up—and more about the opportunity to reach someone in the audience who needs that special something that only I can give them in the moment they need it most. Maybe it's a word of encouragement, or the offer I make that will help them take their business to the next level—or maybe it's something as simple as a smile to let them know that I see them, they are visible to me, and they matter.

So when it comes to visibility, the best definition, in my opinion, is this: "In meteorology, **visibility** is a measure of the distance at which an object or light can be clearly discerned" (Wikipedia).

When my clients double their income or achieve multiple-six-figure weekend events with the programs we have created, it's not about the money—it's about the distance from which their light is able to be seen. It's about creating a bigger impact, changing lives, and shining an ever brighter light into the world so that more people can find their way.

And that's why I speak. That's why I fight through nerves, the fears, and the voices in my head that constantly tell me I should just go back into hiding. It's to give you the tools you need to magnify YOUR light so that you can be seen from an even greater distance by those who need you most.

My encouragement to you today is this: Take that first step, shaking all over, sick to your stomach, and scared to death if need be, because your life matters—the programs, products, and services you offer are a lifeline to those who need you most. YOU have been called to a higher purpose, and now it's your responsibility to step up and step out in faith and say YES to being the light, clearly visible to those you have been called to serve! It's your time to SHINE!

Natalie Lavelock, RN-MSN, is a sought-after program development specialist and online business strategist who works with professional coaches and speakers to create lucrative coaching programs, courses, and certification programs that allow them to scale their business and fully live a life they love.

www.natalielavelock.com

CREATING WORLD-CLASS PARADIGM SHIFTS

Stories That Shift the
Power of Our Thinking

DR. LYDIE LOUIS, PH.D. ESQ.

Star Power!

I could not breathe.

The more I struggled to take a breath, the more it hurt. My eyes stung. My lungs burned. My mouth was wide open, but there was no air. *Someone, anyone, please help me . . . I cannot breathe. I am dying.*

No one came to save me.

Then suddenly I heard someone call my name. "Lydie? Hello, Lydie? Are you okay? You are up next, dear. We are all rooting for you. You will be the first girl to win the New York City Third Grade Regional Competition in years! Go Brooklyn!"

It was worse than I thought. I was not dying. I was a substitute! A first runner-up.

Anthony "the fathead" D'Aganstano, the international boy of mystery, got sick over the weekend with a severe case of mono. Who gets mononucleosis at the age of nine? The principal explained that as the first runner-up, I would represent the school at the regional competition because Anthony was sick. *No, Anthony isn't sick; he's a nincompoop,* I thought.

The principal continued, "The competition begins in two hours in the auditorium."

I absolutely have to get out of here! I am not ready. As I walked to the auditorium, I resigned myself that my only way out of this was prayer. "Dear God, this is me, Lydie. I need your help. Please do not allow me to disgrace myself in front of hundreds of people. Create a wormhole, and I will forever be grateful. Amen."

As I walked on to the stage and stared at the sea of eager, smiling, nameless faces, I knew for certain that I was doomed.

"Lydie? I am Mr. Horton. You are our first contestant today. It is an honor to be at your school which is hosting the competition this year. I also understand that you are the only girl competitor this year. Good luck, young lady!"

"Lydie, the first word of the competition is *enough*. Please provide the panel with the proper spelling of the word *enough*."

"Okay, sir. *Enough* is spelled E-N-U-F."

There was a collective gasp across the auditorium. No one moved. Then slowly those in the audience began to shake their heads. I stood there frozen in my own shame.

"I am sorry, Lydie, that is incorrect. I am not permitted to give you another word. Please leave the stage and join your classmates in the audience." I was humiliated. *Damn Anthony and his silly mononucleosis!*

Then suddenly, I heard a commotion. *Yes, God is creating a wormhole!*

"Stay right there, Lydie! You are not done yet!" A heated discussion transpired between the panel, the principal, and the robust gentlemen with the thick glasses and very nice pinstriped suit.

Then the gentleman with the thick glasses and suit came toward me. He said, "Lydie, I am an attorney with the NYC Board of Education. I am monitoring the spelling competition to ensure accuracy and fairness to all participants. I observed the panel's engagement with you, and there was a fatal error made on the part of the panel that unfairly prejudiced your answer. To cure the fatal error, you will be permitted to continue with the competition. Are you ready for your next spelling word?"

What is happening? "Sir, I get a second chance?"

"Yes, you do."

"But why? How? Are you a wormhole?"

"Lydie, I don't know about a wormhole, but I do know that the panel has to give you a word to spell and also use the word in a sentence to give you context. They must put the word in perspective for you before you attempt to spell the word."

"They did not give you a sentence when they asked you to spell the word *enough*. As such, it is a fatal flaw on the part of the panel, and the only way to cure a fatal flaw is to give you a second chance regardless of how you spelled the word. So, are you ready to continue with the spelling competition?"

Ooh! I was so excited! I felt like I had the power of the stars, and that energy propelled me forward for three continuous days and twenty-seven rounds of the spelling competition. At the end, there can be only one winner, and it was me! *I won!* I was the first girl to win the New York City Regional Spelling Bee Competition in six years! *Girl Power Is Star Power!* "Someone should put that on a T-shirt to remind everyone how awesome girls are!" Oh wait, we did at www.JoyofStarPower.com.

Retirement Power!

There is just something about retirement that frightens us.

We worry that we will not have enough to live on until the end of our days.

We are right. Research shows that most North Americans, including our Canadian and Mexican neighbors, will simply not have enough money in personal savings or retirement to live out our lives in a happy, carefree manner. We will need some sort of governmental supplement to our income, healthcare, and housing. Why is that?

It's because no one taught us the necessary tools, mindset, and commitment to build wealth or come really close to it. We were taught to get a "good" job, save 10 percent, invest a little "depending on our risk tolerance" (whatever that means), and retire at age sixty-five. All lies!

What we've been taught is simply not true. We have to do some critical things if we want to have a comfortable and happy retirement. And we should begin now!

There are some things that you should do yourself, like brushing your teeth, dancing, and planning your retirement—because it's always a little awkward when others do it for you. The key is that you have to *learn it and do it for yourself* with some guidance from experts that you trust. You cannot delegate your retirement power to someone else. It has to come from you.

Can you appreciate that by the time you retire, you will be smarter than you have been your entire life? *Awesome!* You will have done more, seen more, and experienced more than your parents ever could have. Honor them by learning and doing what you need to do make your retirement powerful. Let's do a paradigm shift to re-imagine and redesign your retirement power.

Here are the principal things you should begin to focus on:

1. Learn how to safely invest and preserve your retirement income so that it's always there.
2. Start a small business now that brings you happiness and income—you will need both.
3. Own a little real estate that can provide you with both housing and a rental income.
4. Figure out social media—your digital media assets are your world-class perpetual assets that should be monetized to fund your retirement.

You can do this!

Be consistent. Work with the right experts. Be brave and build a brilliant business for your future to create a world-class retirement and beyond.

If you would like to join a community of business entrepreneurs who are building a world-class retirement, I invite you to join www. JoyofSuccess360.com.

We get together bi-monthly to share what's working, what's not, and what we need to do now for Our Vision, Our Value, Our Visibility.

Legacy Power!

Death has a way of changing us.

We are humbled. We are saddened. We fear our own fragility and mortality.

And, perhaps more importantly, we wonder whether we have fulfilled our purpose.

You are not alone in these thoughts. But what will you do differently to ensure that your business, assets, and loved ones can continue to benefit after you have gone? In other words, how do you create your legacy?

Legacies are not only for the rich. They are for everyone. There are many models of legacies. Examples include the Rockefeller Trust, the Getty Trust, the Jones' Family Trust, and the Dr. Lydie Trust. These trusts are specifically designed to carry on the wishes of the persons that created them, regardless of what those wishes are—including feeding the homeless, providing money to various charities or to your family, preservation of real estate, and stock holdings. The trust(s) will continue for as long as there are assets to fund the trust. Your dream(s) will live on.

So how do you fund a trust? In every possible way you can. The best way, however, is with a life insurance policy. The proceeds of a life insurance policy can be used for a trust that will continue to provide financing for your dreams as well as a stream of TAX-FREE income for your family for many generations to come.

You can learn more about building a legacy and the power of insurance at www.joyoflegacy.com.

I hope these ministories have shifted your thinking and empowered you to see your life in a deeper meaningfully richer paradigm. I am on a mission to create one million millionaires world-wide by 2035. Join me on this journey!

Dr. Lydie Louis, Ph.D. Esq. is The Money & Law Doctor. She is a philanthropist and venture capitalist. A New York City business attorney, law professor, and business mentor. She is an internationally recognized expert on business strategy, intellectual property, and wealth creation. She has been featured in the *Wall Street Journal, New York Times*, and *USA Today*. Bob Circosta has crowned Dr. Lydie "The Suze Orman of Law." Dr. Lydie is the host of The Money, Law & You Podcast.

www.drlydie.com

SPIRIT: YOUR PATH TO THE GREATEST IMPACT

SID MCNAIRY

When I walk in a room, I introduce myself and love to dive right in. The drive for success is what keeps me going, but it also has often led to burnout. There is a cost in this way of living that took some time for me to understand. I came from playing sports, and at seven years old, I had the desire to win. That strong desire stayed with me and eventually took me into coaching Division I football, traveling around the country, and looking for the next win. After twelve years of coaching, helping turn four different university teams from losers to winners, I found myself at a loss. I was sick of the person I was becoming on the inside—the person that was costing me the relationships in my life.

When I was eight years old, I had begun to meditate with my soccer coach, and it stayed with me. When I was coaching football, yoga found me when a lady noticed that I needed to heal my physical body. She never warned me that yoga would eventually take me out of football. And that is where the shift from powerhouse football coach putting players in the NFL to world-renowned yoga instructor began.

Yoga became my next stage to win on. I would spend the next fifteen years gaining more accolades away from the game. Becoming a best-selling author, teaching classes with hundreds of people in the room, and speaking on stages to help others find peace and reach for enlightenment all gave me credit in the yoga world. I spent my days traveling the world, training yoga teachers, and opening yoga studios—until suddenly one day yoga became more stressful than I could ever remember football being.

I realized that I was seventy-five pounds heavier, and I found myself missing that sense of peace once again.

This may seem familiar for many of you achievers in the world; in fact, you may be experiencing the exact feeling I'm describing. Burnout was the common denominator of the "win at all cost" mentality that drove me to be a coach, yogi, singer-songwriter, artist, father, and more.

In 2017 I began to realize that I was dying on the inside. I was stuck in bed, and somehow I knew everything needed to shift. The next two years would cause me to take a deep look within to see what was next. My wife and I made the decision to sell everything and hit the road in April 2019.

Over those two years of healing, I began learning what it was to be grounded in self-love. The steps I took moved me forward and helped me to uncover my best self in every way. A major lesson was looking within and seeing my own self-worth. Beyond the need to be in the limelight, what did I have that I could value, no matter what I was doing or where I was? It was a powerful place to be in.

The second step came from changing my inner dialogue. I took the time to celebrate me and watch how those around me would celebrate me as well. Then it was time to put it all into action.

What many did not know when I was coaching football or teaching yoga was that I was often in the midst of thousands of people yet still felt alone. We all have programs—patterns that we have to protect ourselves from old traumas that we experience either consciously or unconsciously. When I saw my programs, it was time to get free. One major goal that came up for me was to open up to relationships, no matter where I was.

This was the real key to success in my life. How could I build my relationship with my wife and live my best life? How could I build my relationship with my kids and family? How could I be the friend I was yearning for? I would have to become vulnerable and let people see all of me.

That was the secret sauce to my greatest shift. I would let others in and see what was possible when I was fully available beyond my scars of yesterday.

Get real and see it all heal!

Once that statement landed in my bones, the world opened up a new door for me to go through. *Get real and see it all heal.* I would look at everything going forward and see where I could help myself, knowing that this ultimately would help me to help others. I saw my wounds heal, and I saw the people around me doing the same for themselves.

The lessons that came to me as my wife and I drove across the country were incredible. It was my time in the desert, and out of this so much came forth. The content for my book *Those Who Know God* came to me in three days, and I knew I was ready to transform my relationships—and that included my relationship with myself.

One major lesson I've learned is to STOP, LISTEN, and FEEL. This process helped me to see how to clear away old patterns while opening myself up to what was next.

As you can imagine, spending a year on the road takes a great deal of discipline. The discipline I learned in sports was a major lesson along the way, and if I was going to make it through this, discipline was going to be my fuel. I chose to take this time to create new habits, heal myself, lose those seventy-five pounds, and start anew no matter where I found myself. It comes down to discipline—be willing to be that for yourself.

Another powerful lesson I learned is an oldie but a goodie: acceptance. Acceptance is the greatest form of love we can give to another person and to ourselves. This one came up several times, and it was amazing. The more I have been willing to let go of being right and have accepted things as they are, the happier I've become.

So let me ask you: What will it be—will you continue to need to be right or will you choose to accept where things are and find happiness through gratitude in all things?

When my wife and I finally landed in our new home, many doors opened. The biggest has been the door of collaboration. In football, many see opposing teams as competition first, while in truth these teams are a brotherhood, where even years after the game is over, many who participated in the game stand for each other. It was love that elevated all those involved, no matter how many times we would stand across the field from one another. My love for those in the game still continues to grow today.

It took me stepping away to realize that what we have is a brotherhood. Today my goal is to expand the level of brotherhood to all those in the game of life, no matter who they are. It is in elevating others into their greatness that lifts each of us to new heights.

In coaching we are invited to share in our expertise with the players we coach. I am reminded of my first speech as a football coach. On the way to speak, my head coach at Northern Illinois University, Joe Novak, said, "Just make sure you give them one thing to use and that it is a great gift." I have gone on to give many speeches, and I still look to share one nugget to keep everyone going forward. That is what it is all about. We all have something unique inside of us, and it is up to us to find it and share it with the world.

Keep going—it is all inside of you. When you are ready, we can find it together.

Sid McNairy is the founder and lead wellness instructor of Nahi Wellness and the author of three books: *Yoga and Life Empowerment, The Warrior Within,* and *Those Who Know God.* Leaving a lucrative career as a college football coach, his work has taken him around the world as a mindset coach, life empowerment coach, healer, leader of meditation, instructor of yoga, and inspirational teacher.

www.sidmcnairy.com

SAY YES!

SHERYL PLOUFFE

I'm lumbering across the stage in high heels that don't feel like my own—because they're not. Thankfully my seventeen-year-old feet are about the same size as my mom's. These are the only fancy shoes we own between us. My dress is a vintage 1950's silk A-line from the Salvation Army that we bought for three dollars. My mom gently and painstakingly hand-sewed sequins on it to make it sparkle and look less second-hand. I reach the emcee and look at the crowd of about four hundred or so parents, grandparents, teachers, and pageant-supporters in the auditorium. Here comes my semi-final question.

I wish I could tell you today, thirty-two years later, what that question was, but it's a blur. It was probably something like "How would you make the world a better place?" What isn't a blur, though, is the feeling I had on stage at the moment when the audience gasped. I answered the question as any aspiring Miss Teen Nanaimo should, but then I asked if I could answer the question again—this time in French.

I'm from a mid-size mining town in northern Ontario, Canada, where bilingualism is not an anomaly. My family moved to British Columbia in 1984, and it turns out that speaking French on the West Coast is a stand-out skill. So, in true pageant fashion, I decided to use everything I had to try to win this competition.

I answered the question in French to roaring applause, although only a few people understood a word I said. I placed First Runner-Up that day, but it didn't matter that I didn't win the top prize. I felt like a winner.

I haven't always felt that way. When we moved to BC, my mom was separated from my dad and had four kids under twelve to take care of. We lived below the poverty line throughout my teen years, and I was painfully shy as a kid. If the teacher called on me in class, I'd feel the heat of everyone's eyes on me, and I would sometimes burst into tears.

So how did a shy, insecure French-Canadian girl from the wrong side of town eventually become a national TV broadcaster, college professor, news manager, and entrepreneur?

It all started when I was fifteen. A school friend asked a whole group of us if we'd be interested in modeling in a local fashion show. Her mom was part of a knitting group looking to show off their artisanal scarves, sweaters, and berets.

I don't know what came over me, but I said yes.

Soon it was showtime. I stood behind the wall partition, waiting for my turn to walk the runway in front of about twenty-five people at the local clay and glass gallery, and I was trembling. But I did it! I walked, pivoted just like we practiced, and smiled back at the audience.

When I returned to change into my next outfit, I was still nervous, but noticeably not as nervous as the first time. Ten outfits later, I was thrilled. Not that the show was over, but that I had faced my fear.

This became a pattern. I sought opportunities to relive that feeling of confidence, worth, and belonging.

By the time I was eighteen, I was hosting a weekly cable TV show that reached tens of thousands of people.

I had been volunteering at the local cable station as part of the studio crew pulling cables and operating the camera. I started volunteering so that I could put something down on my "résumé" for my bid to become Miss Nanaimo. I was now going to try for the big prize in local pageantry.

One of the producers asked me if I'd be willing to give hosting a try. I said yes.

I still remember the feeling I had the first time I stepped in front of the camera. I didn't know where to look, my palms were sweaty, and my knees were knocking. But I did it! I went on to host that show for close to three years. The TV show helped me beef up my résumé for the upcoming contest, but I also needed to prepare for the talent competition.

I had taken piano and tap dancing lessons until I was six. Those lessons abruptly ended when my dad's business partner at the time took off with all of their money, never to be seen again. So I didn't have a talent I could fall back on.

My mom said, "What if you sing?" I said yes, but with a glimmer of doubt that this would work.

So back to the Salvation Army store we went. We found a seven-dollar black-and-red Spanish-style dress replete with an abundance of ruffles.

Not only would we need way more sequins this time around, but I'd also have to find a singing voice.

I stood behind the heavy 20-foot-tall burgundy velvet curtains of Beban Auditorium, once again ready to take the stage—this time to sing to an instrumental, karaoke version of "La Isla Bonita" by Madonna.

As the curtain parted, my heart was beating outside my chest. They pressed play on the cassette. I strode from one side of the stage to the other, singing into my handheld microphone and looking out into the crowd. Thankfully, all I saw were bright lights.

That evening I became the city's ambassador. I traveled the province, speaking alongside other city dignitaries for the next year. I also won the talent competition. To this day, it's still one of the scariest things I've ever done.

Had it not been for saying yes to any of these opportunities, I wouldn't have gone on to do over 20,000 hours of television broadcasting over the course of my career. I wouldn't now be helping other coaches, consultants, and entrepreneurs to step into the spotlight, speak on camera, and take center stage.

So say yes!

Say yes, despite insecurities, fear, and potential failure. I think you'll find, as I have, that nothing bad comes from saying yes!

Sheryl Plouffe is an entrepreneur, international speaker, and former Canadian TV broadcaster. She has been seen by millions over the course of her twenty-five-year career in news media, has produced thousands of videos, and has broadcast over 20,000 hours of live television. Sheryl lives and works in Ontario, Canada.

http://www.sherylplouffe.com/

BECOMING A GIFTED LEADER

LOUIE SHARP

I am sitting in the briefing room with eleven other Marines. We are going over the day's mission. I am a crew chief and door gunner on UH-1N "Huey" helicopters. Today we will be inserting grunts (i.e., infantrymen) into different LZs (landing zones). I have been assigned to fly with Lieutenant Colonel Bill Nerbun as the PIC (Pilot in Command) and Captain Bill Morhardt as his copilot. We are going to be dash 4 (-4) of the flight of four helicopters—we would be the last helicopter in the flight and the last one to go into all the LZs.

During the briefing, I look over at Bill. He is always prepared, calm, focused, and professional. He has blue-gray eyes that always have a sparkle in them. I cannot get over how he looks more like a computer programmer or an accountant than a Marine aviator. My first thought is, *Why did I get stuck with this guy?* Then the next thought pops into my head. *If the "stuff" is going to hit the fan, I would want this guy at the controls of the helicopter.* He is always low-key, positive, hardworking, funny, and calm. I have never seen him lose his composure.

As we walk out to the helicopter for the preflight before launch, I tell Col. Nerburn that he is an amazing leader with several gifts that I really admire.

The mission is going as expected. Around midday we are directed to start inserting the grunts into a different LZ. On our final approach to the new LZ, the first helicopter, dash 1, radios back for dash 3 and dash 4 to wave off and go around the LZ; it's too small to fit four helicopters.

Almost immediately after that radio call, we lose one of our two engines. Normally we would have single-engine fly-away capability. On this day, though, we are already very heavy, slow, and hot, which is giving us less lift. As soon as I realized that we had lost an engine, I heard Bill come over the radio and say, "May Day, May Day, we are going down." What was most amazing was that he said it in a calm and collected manner. He then took the controls back from the copilot.

Helicopters cannot glide—they autorotate, which basically means it's a controlled crash. We are at 700 feet when we lose our engine—the equivalent to a seventy-story building. We are flying over a forest, and Col. Nerburn finds the only safe spot to land. We hit so hard that the helicopter bounces twenty-five feet into the air, rolls to the left, and crashes into the ground for the second, and last, time.

By the grace of God, we all live. I am the second-to-the-last to be released from the hospital. Only Bill is left. I go to his room with the intention of thanking him for saving my life. There is no doubt in my mind that his quick actions, calmness, and levelheaded response saved all of our lives. When I get to his room, they have him propped up. He was the only one still upright on impact. It is obvious he is in a great amount of pain. As I look into his eyes, they still have that amazing sparkle in them. I find myself at a loss for words. How do you thank someone for literally physically saving your life? As our eyes meet, I know he under-stands what I want to say but cannot. After some small talk, I start to leave. Before I get to the door, Bill stops me and says, "Louie, you are a gifted leader too." This is the first time I hear these two words put together in that order. As I leave the hospital that day, I silently commit to myself and to Bill that I will become a gifted leader.

***

Today when I speak to corporations, businesses, and organizations, I first ask, "Who in the room is a leader?" Most hands go up. I explain that we are all leaders regardless of our jobs or anything else in our lives. Someone is always watching us, even if it is pumping gas at the gas station. Each of us is a leader. Then I ask: "By a show of hands, who has made a positive impact on the life of another person?" Every hand in the room goes up. This makes all of us Gifted Leaders!

I am going to share with you two key skills I have learned about leadership and how they can help you grow your business, teams, or organization for more proficiency, productivity, and profit.

1. Be brave. The first thing I would like to share is the importance of being brave enough to be "Younique" in the marketplace. The purpose of your YSP (Younique Selling Proposition) is to literally make you Younique compared to everybody else in your market. Your ability to be totally unique is NOT based on how long you have been in business or how great your client care is. It is not based on you, your education, your story, or anything else about you. It is ALL about your clients. Being Younique is based on how well you solve the challenges, problems, and issues of your target market clients. Until you understand this, you will spend more time, energy, and money than you need to for the results you are after.

Nike and State Farm Insurance are great examples of this. What makes them unique in the marketplace? NOTHING! Instead they are spending literally billions of dollars to buy the market.

As a gifted leader, it is your responsibility to find out:

- The top three to four problems your target market faces
- The solutions to your target market's top problems
- The best way to deliver the message of your YSP to your target market

This is true whether you own the company, are a solopreneur, or manage a team in a company.

I was consulting for a company that was struggling to define their Younique Selling Proposition. After I helped them figure out who their target market was, we got busy getting clear on their YSP. We discovered that their ideal client struggled with time, inconvenience, and a lack of knowledge of what to do when they had a need for that company's services. We then developed the solutions to ALL those problems. Next, we communicated that to the target market. By doing this, this company became more profitable, more productive, and more proficient. They spent less time, less energy, and less money, and they increased their business.

Bill Nerbun was both brave and Younique. He did not dress or look like anyone else. But when it came time to deliver, he was *priceless*!

2. Take care of the troops. Nobody has ever accomplished anything on their own. They have all been supported by others and worked with others. You, your company, your organization, and your team are no different. Here are a couple of ways to take care of your troops.

1. Lead by wandering around. Yep, that's right—go wander around. (And, yes, this IS possible even if your team works remotely.) The purpose of your wandering around is twofold:
    a. First, look for something they are doing well and give them genuine, positive appreciation.
    b. Second, get to know them better. Build your relationship with them. I can tell you what is going on in the personal lives of all my employees right now. Building relationships with your team will give YOU great insight into what they are struggling with and how it is affecting their work. You do not have to have the answers. They just want to know that you care.
    c. Third, write down the names of everybody on your team. Could you buy a book for each of your employees based on their individual interests, needs, hobbies, likes, goals, and passions? If not, this would be a great first step to help you become more acquainted with your team.
2. Let go of taking anything personally. When people screw up, upset you, and disappoint you, remember that it has nothing to do with you. When you realize that everybody is doing the best they can with where they are, it changes the game of leadership completely.

In the United States Marine Corps, they teach that the two most important things in leadership are to accomplish the mission and to take care of the troops. Being brave, the first gifted leadership trait I shared, accomplishes the mission to grow your organization, your team, and your company faster with less time, energy, and money. The second gifted leadership trait is taking care of your troops. There has been plenty of research and studies proving that happy, connected people are more productive, proficient, and profitable.

For your FREE eleven strategies to build your YSP, email info@ thegiftedleader.com. Using these strategies, you'll be a truly Younique and gifted leader!

Louie Sharp is an international, world-class keynote speaker. He has been seen on ABC, NBC, delivered keynote speeches for DuPont, Edward Jones, Sage, Fender, and Axalta, and has shared the stage with Jack Canfield! He started his first company at age twenty-three, and thirty-nine years later, it is still going strong.

www.thegiftedleader.com

THE TREASURE IN THE DARKNESS THAT DEFIES LOGIC!

DR. ALEXANDRA SITCH

B ack in the eighties, right out of school, I dreamed of a life full of travel and different cultures. I have always felt like a fish in the water with my extremely diverse group of friends around the world.

I studied international relations, languages, and conflict resolution, and I loved to switch from one language to another and connect different people during negotiations and other professional situations. I worked in peace-building organizations and NGOs, and I also had some great international communication jobs, including the European Commission, Westin Hotels, Air France/KLM/Delta Airlines, and French German Railways.

On a personal level, I experienced a turbulent love relationship. I gave up a brilliant sales director job in the Burgundy area of France, where I had done presentations and incentives regarding Burgundy history, culture, and wines. Now with this new partner, I had already planned out our new life in my mind: a life in the Highlands, managing character hotels and haunted castles and offering them to travel agents. It sounded wonderful, although my intuition told me there was something not right.

Well, my professional life worked out, but my love life did not.

Completely heartbroken and doubting myself, I had to take a break from my work and turn inward. I noticed that the most interesting journey of all was going deep down into the dark chambers of my soul.

I asked myself, "Who am I? What do I really want to do in this world? Do I want to continue chasing unavailable partners and fit into a life full of control? Or could I embrace my vulnerable side, have faith in the waves of life, and listen to my intuition and heart—going for innovative visions and relations that really fit me?"

Solving conflicts and misunderstandings in different environments had been my specialty, but inner conflicts were unknown terrain for me. I began to dive into psychology books and energy work. One day, I visited an equine-assisted coaching congress. I had always been around horses, and I knew their magical power and wisdom. They showed me a mirror of myself, my relationships, and my place in life during one of the sessions. The horses came closer when I made an inner movement and would stay at a distance if I was not really my authentic self. I discovered how much animals and their energy can help us in our conflicts. They can show us the systemic influences that stem from the past, even from past generations, and from our childhood. It is this heart intelligence that is essential; when you use your entire body as an organ of perception, you embrace the world and sense your place in it more deeply, guiding you toward a new balance.

I trained in equine-assisted and shamanic life and healing coaching and worked with individuals as well as insurance firms, banks, women's associations, and psychotherapists all over Europe and the Middle East. I saw how much it empowers managers, teams, and individuals to improve their nonverbal communication and focus on their intuition and authenticity—the treasure in the darkness.

This method embraces both the heart and the mind and works with nature to find your inner compass, and her power to heal and gain insight! The following is an excerpt from my bestselling book *The Universal Language of Nature*:

> Intuitively, Cybil knew that the two horses looking into the distance were their children; they stood a little farther away and had begun to move, meanwhile. She "saw" her husband in a different horse standing on the other side, a little separated; the man in person had intuitively added himself.
>
> I asked her which horses she felt most attracted to and whether she could go there. She walked to the horses that

represented her children. The moment she walked to them, the horses moved a little farther away, totally focused on other things. This happened again and again as Cybil began to move and attempted to seek contact with the horses.

"What do you feel because of that?" I asked her. She became thoughtful and looked a bit perplexed. It felt like she was getting in their way or as if she somehow would hassle them. "I'm always a bit worried. In fact, my daughter often tells me to give her a little more room to do her things.

"Oh!" Cybil said suddenly. "I think they are very happy, and without any worries, they are able to follow their life."

"And what about your own life?" I asked her. She was very quiet and had to admit that, in fact, she did not have one. "I'm not sure where I belong anymore," she said.

Cybil saw that the horse representing her husband was still standing motionless beside the stables.

"He's also like that horse, totally absorbed in other things, just not the kids or me. I think he's going to have a burnout, the way he lives," she said, a bit bitterly.

For a moment, I did not know what to say. I tried to find answers, torturing my mind. There was a blank. Then I realized that the answer lay in the "not knowing," in setting aside expectations of being the "ideal" me. And suddenly there was a movement, and the answer unfolded!

Nature was quiet again, and the mare, which represented Cybil, suddenly moved to one of the women present, stopped there, and pointed at her to come into the field.

"That's weird," Cybil said. "I was just about to ask her."

The woman, who represented her heart, walked into the field and stopped far away from Cybil. "Why do you want to stand here, heart of Cybil?" I asked.

"I cannot go on," she said. "I have to keep my distance, away from her."

"Does that tell you something?" I asked Cybil.

"Yes, I cannot get in touch with what I really, profoundly want. I'm alien to myself." She cried and stood, a bit lost, in the middle.

"Could you walk to your heart and make a new contact with it?"

It was fascinating how much this representative could feel the energy and emotions of the heart, even if she did not know the person at all. This is the deep body-knowledge, the sensitivity to energy, the intuition that all of us carry within ourselves.

Tears streamed down her cheeks as Cybil looked into the eyes of her heart and they held hands. She had the feeling of finding herself again. The mare came and tenderly put her nose on both hands to seal that energy.

The right words are important and provide a whole new energy and dynamism that influence a person's system and behavior: "I am your heart, and I only beat for you; never let go of me and listen to me.

"You are my heart, and you are just beating for me; I will always carry you and be with you."

By now, the mare was standing motionless by her and her "heart" and in between her and her husband. Then, the very moment Cybil made contact with her heart, the other "children" horses came closer to her again, which she immediately noticed. When she turned her attention from her heart to her husband, the mare moved to the side and opened the way to her husband.

As they walked toward each other, the energy was very different. Since Cybil had taken the first step to owning her own power and potential, to her heart, and was able to let go—in this case, of her worries about her children—her husband could also feel freer to develop his authentic power and establish a new relationship.[1]

This session taught me that often the treasure lies in the darkness! Letting go of control, cherishing unconditional self-love, and flowing with the waves of life give us a certain power. As a mediator and coach, I really had moments during this session of just not "knowing." At the

---

[1](From my bestselling book: *The Universal Language of Nature: A New Way of Conflict Resolution and Authentic Leadership*, (New York: Hybrid Global Publishing, 2020).

moment I admitted this and just trusted in that which is, the answer came to me naturally!

I know now that my heart and body wisdom are part of the interconnectivity between beings and can put things into motion. They allow me to be authentic and transmit the right message or offer the appropriate help.

My journey started with the collective, but it has developed into a life path of going back to myself and going back to the individual in order to create more consciousness and therefore a more harmonious society.

Having faith in the waves of life and faith in yourself attracts the right situations, speaker possibilities, job opportunities, people, and relations. What appears to your conscious mind as darkness is simply the unknown—a fruitful realm of untapped possibility. You, as a divine being, can be the creator within that space. Dancing with uncertainty raises your confidence and allows you to collaborate with the greater mysteries of life!

Dr. Alexandra Sitch speaks eight languages fluently and has worked as an interpreter, international conflict mediator, and life and healing coach throughout Europe and the Middle East. She lives in France and regularly speaks at international conferences and organizes mediation, equine-assisted life coaching, and self-empowerment workshops across Europe and the US. Alexandra is the bestselling author of the book *The Universal Language of Nature.*

www.sitchmediation.com

THE BEST PART

JASE SOUDER

The first time I spoke and sold my own seminars and coaching, I made ninety-eight thousand dollars in sales. The second time I spoke and sold my own seminars and coaching, I made about four thousand dollars. The third time, I made about forty thousand. The fourth time, I made just a few thousand.

Then one day, I made zero.

That doesn't mean I broke even; I had to pay for my own travel and expenses, so I lost money. But losing money wasn't the worst part.

What was worse is that I had no idea why I sometimes crushed it and sometimes sold nothing. The big sales days were great; taking home tens of thousands of dollars from one speech tided me over the times when I sold poorly, but the ups and downs were frustrating. There was no continuity, and my confidence started to take a beating. But even that wasn't the worst part.

I started my career working for one of the best speakers, and I watched him sell from the stage over and over again. When he finally gave me a shot, he said, "You've seen me do it enough times. Go do it." That literally was the extent of my training.

I got a copy of his presentation and attempted to memorize it word for word, but it was his speech, so I couldn't duplicate it exactly. I couldn't tell his stories either; that would have been inauthentic.

The first time I spoke and sold his stuff, I did ninety-six thousand dollars in sales. But I didn't have any idea why it worked, so the next time I did under fifty thousand in sales, and then the next time even less. I had no idea what I was doing.

Next I started selling my own seminars, and I worked at getting better. I paid one guy four thousand dollars just to learn to close. I paid another guy twenty-five thousand dollars to help me write a presentation. I invested a lot of money, but there still was no consistency. But even *that* wasn't the worst part.

When you're selling from stage, as I was, the promoter gets a percentage of your sales. At that time, the standard was 50 percent, so if I sold forty thousand dollars in seminars, the promoter would get twenty thousand. Promoters look at their guest speaking slots as revenue-generating opportunities, and if there were little-to-no sales, it costs them money. If one speaker could make them twenty thousand dollars and another makes them zero, it's a big difference. So, if a speaker sells poorly, the promoter isn't happy. But that's still not the worst part.

Promoters are part of a tight network, and they talk. If a speaker bombs on one stage, the promoters tell the other promoters to stay away, so bombing on stage costs the speaker the opportunity to get on other stages. Yet even that wasn't the worst part.

One day I spoke at an event where I'd spoken previously and hadn't done too well. I wasn't confident. I still couldn't count on my speaking to generate sales; I didn't know what made it work. I just hoped that if I was on, excited, and resonated with the audience, they'd buy.

I did my best—and made zero sales. I was disheartened and out a good chunk of change since I'd paid for travel and lodging for my assistant and myself. The promoter sent his assistant to take us to dinner, and I thought, *Oh, maybe the promoter told his assistant to give me a pep talk.*

The promoter's assistant was acting awkwardly, and about halfway through the meal, he looked at me. "We'd like to invite you . . ." he said, and then after a big pause, "not to come back."

That was the worst part.

I was embarrassed, I was hurt, and I was a bit ashamed. I'd put my heart and money into learning to get better, my speaking was about something very important to me, I wanted to make money, and more importantly I wanted to make a difference for the audience—and now I was invited not to come back.

That stung, and I was worried that the word would get out that I bombed, and other stages would disappear.

I had to do something about it, so I kept signing up for speaker trainings, investing in leadership and development trainings, and working on my craft, but my sales stayed inconsistent. Until the recession—when all sales stopped.

The market for my seminars and coaching was real estate investors. I was teaching them personal growth and one-to-one sales. I'd mastered one-to-one sales, but that doesn't translate to one-to-many. When the recession of 2007 happened, the real estate market dried up fast, and the demand for training real estate investors disappeared.

While this was devastating to my business, it turned into a blessing for me. Suddenly I had a lot of time on my hands.

I was thinking and praying about how I could continue to serve people and make it more affordable and effective for them to learn. I decided to take the best of my $2,500 seminar and create a home study course on sales.

I had been teaching sales for years, and I wanted to get even better. In order to make the best product I could, I threw myself into learning sales. I started reading more sales books, watching videos, and binging on TED Talks. I spent hours watching these talks on YouTube.

The talks that really impacted me were the ones on social dynamics and psychology. I learned about what creates lifelong fans and clients, what triggers unconscious social networks, and what causes masses of people to take action.

About this time, I had the desire to figure out a system for speaking. I asked myself, "What am I doing when I rock? What am I not doing when I bomb? How can I consistently make sales?" I realized the principles I was learning about sales, social dynamics, and psychology could be applied to writing speeches and presentations that move people to action.

I combined my learning, experiences, and training and created a system—a framework for writing high-converting speeches. I realized that there are a series of yeses we need to get from the audience in order for them to purchase from us. It's like there are a series of light switches, and they must all be switched into the on position, in the correct order, in order for the light bulb to go on and our audience to say yes to our offer.

To make sure all the switches were on in every presentation, I created a repeatable system I could follow to write my presentations. It wasn't a template of words or sentences to say—instead it was a series of discussions and stories to tell in order to activate and move the audience.

Soon after I finished producing my home study course on sales and creating this framework for speaking, I was given an opportunity to audition, or "try out," for a big stage. The audition came with a catch: I wasn't allowed to sell. The promoter put this in the contract and kept saying, "Remember, you're not allowed to sell."

The day for the audition came. I used the template, and I rocked the presentation. The audience was engaged; they laughed, they were inspired, and they gave me a standing ovation.

At the end of the presentation, the promoter walked on stage and whispered in my ear, "Let's sell your stuff."

I replied, "I thought I wasn't allowed to sell." He said, "You rocked it; let's sell your stuff—we'll give them a discount."

We sold my home study course, and that one day's sales, even after discounting the price, equaled 25 percent of my previous year's sales!

After the event, the attendees left and the promoter asked me to sit and talk. After a couple minutes of small talk, he looked at me and said, "I'd like to invite you . . ." My heart felt like it stopped. I thought I did well; I thought he'd be happy. The last time I heard that phrase, it didn't end well. Then he continued, ". . . to speak to my group four times a year; I'll pay you a monthly retainer to do it, and you can sell your stuff every time, including being on stage at my big three-hundred-person event."

Using the system I created, I spoke at his big event, and that one day's sales equaled 50 percent of my prior year's income. With two speeches using my new speaking system, I made sales equal to 75 percent of my previous year's income, and I spoke on his stage for the next seven years.

I've gone on to speak on multiple stages, create hundreds of thousands of dollars in sales, and impact hundreds of lives.

That was the best part.

Jase Souder believes that you have a God-given mission and it can be fulfilled and funded through your business. Jase founded the World Class Speaker Academy to help entrepreneurs change the world by becoming World Class Speakers who create massive impact, raving fans, and a rush of new clients with every presentation.

www.worldclassspeakeracademy.com

THE 1-MINUTE TALK: THE SECRET TO REVENUE GROWTH IN A DISTRACTED WORLD

MARINA STAMOS

The average person in the US is exposed to between 4,000 and 10,000 ads per day.

—*Forbes, New York Times*

Have you ever watched someone give a talk about the work they do—and it is simply *fantastic*? The audience members look up from their phones, lean in to the speaker, and hang on every word. When the speaker invites people to connect, the audience rushes to meet them, hungry for more.

Does that sound familiar?

Have you ever watched someone give a talk about the work they do—and it is *not fantastic*? It's a total fail. Heck, it's painful to watch. You feel sorry for the speaker, but you can't stop yourself from looking down at your phone to avoid making eye contact. Or you totally tune the speaker out and go back to scrolling on your phone, fielding texts, alerts, pop-ups, and more, while their voice fades to a distant white noise in the background. Either way, that speaker has made themselves invisible. When they offer to connect with the audience after the talk . . . crickets.

Does that also sound familiar?

The worst case of a "not fantastic" talk happened a few years ago in an elegantly appointed conference room in downtown Philadelphia, Pennsylvania.

The speaker?

Me.

I was giving my first public talk about my communications company and how I helped business owners use powerful messaging to grow their influence and income.

At least, that was what I was *trying* to say. Instead, I was a rambling, fumbling, no-message mess.

I still recall the pang of embarrassment when I saw audience members looking down at their phones to avoid making eye contact with me.

At the end of my talk, I met the gaze of the event host. She managed to force a conflicted, mechanical smile—like an emoji gif executing a preprogrammed action that I read as "At least you tried. Now please, go away."

This should have been a no-brainer.

I was an Emmy-nominated television news producer who had spent years in the messaging trenches, turning thousands of wide-eyed, hopeful unknowns into highly visible, important, newsworthy stars in the eyes of millions. (I get the irony—I could do it for others, but when it came to doing for myself, not so much.)

Clients paid five thousand, thirty-five thousand, even fifty-five thousand dollars and more for my expertise. I helped them achieve massive revenue growth, and their successes were featured everywhere from the TEDx stage to the *Oprah Magazine*.

Here's the thing, though. These were all "accidental clients," ones I'd meet casually at a party or through a family member or friend. That was a terrible strategy, and I knew it. But I was stuck, blocked, and confused about how to talk about my business.

As you can imagine, there were a lot of zero-dollar months.

Now I have a lot of five thousand dollar days (and more).

How?

A secret formula I call the 1-Minute Talk.™

As I dragged myself home after my ill-fated talk, racked with confusion and regret, I knew that something had to change. I didn't know how to talk about my work in a quick and powerful manner. I sat down with a yellow notepad, and I promised myself that things were going to be different. From that day forward, I was only going to do what worked, and I was going to stop doing what doesn't work.

I thought about my own process—the way I crafted messaging for others. What was I tapping into?

Then one word floated up into my consciousness: *EMOTIONS*.

A Harvard study quoted in *Inc.* magazine says that when it comes to what drives buying behavior, "it's not price, it's emotions." I had read numerous studies of human behavior, from purchasing, voting, mating, and everything in between, and they all could be reduced to emotions.

I knew I had to inspire emotions, such as hope, curiosity, and trust. But now what? How do I operationalize this "emotions thingy"?

All the structures of good messaging are already well established. You can find them everywhere you look. And I was able to harness them for the benefit of others in my sleep. But I needed a new, systematic, and intentional way to make the structures work for me.

I put myself into my niche's shoes and started to ask myself a different set of questions.

HERE'S ONE YOU CAN USE TODAY: What is your niche Googling? That is what they are struggling with and feel hopeless about. Their keywords are your cue to the first words you should use in a profitable talk.

After writing down every discrete step to messaging that had catapulted my clients to success, I saw something staring up at me from the page.

First, the key to powerful messaging was to look behind the words for the key emotions they inspire.

Second, I had to state my value quickly. In one minute, to be exact. Not an elevator pitch, but a fully rendered talk, intentionally crafted to magnetize ideal clients and take them from absolute zero to making an appealing offer—using simple, everyday words that sound like a story, without a hint of jargon, process, or salesy-ness.

That was the moment I created The 1-Minute Talk™ formula.

BEFORE: JARGON, PROCESS AND SALESY-NESS IN THE FIRST WORDS OF A TALK

Who wants to hear about my proven five-STEP R.A.I.S.E. CAREER NAVIGATOR SYSTEM that uses best-practices of Resilience, Agility, Innovation, Self-Care, and Emotional

Intelligence? You'll be amazed at how the system works! It helped my career and salary soar to the greatest heights and can work for you too!

AFTER: STARTING WITH AN EMOTION-INSPIRING STORY

I remember the day my manager called us into the conference room. The promotion—that I secretly wanted—was going to someone else . . . again. I forced a smile. No one likes a sore loser. But behind that smile, I was making a plan. Today, I have my dream job as a senior VP, with double the salary—and that manager answers to me now.

Can you feel the difference? It's the difference between the audience tuning out or leaning in. Money is lost when you use the BEFORE model. Money is made when you use the story-based approach to inspiring emotions. It's that simple.

After twenty years of writing and entrepreneurship, and after testing, failing, testing, and failing again, I created The 1-Minute Talk™ client-attraction system that changed everything for me and my business.

Today, I know how to walk into any room (live or virtual) where my target niche is hanging out and close them on a four-figure package within twenty-four hours of our first encounter.

Most importantly, I help my clients to achieve their first four- and five-figure months (sometimes more) and their six- and seven-figure years. I've helped my clients move from being invisible and barely making twenty dollars an hour for their work to being unforgettable and making five hundred to one thousand dollars per hour and more.

A woman who was in a Zoom networking event during the COVID pandemic heard me give my 1-Minute Talk™ and emailed me saying she wanted to work with me. She is a sixty-something fashion industry expert whose income is driven by commissions on clothing sales and was used to making upwards of $200,000 a year for her work. Now, during quarantine, the bottom had fallen out, and she was at dire financial risk. Prior to our meeting, she relied on one way of talking about her work:

colors, fabrics, textures, and hats. She tended to make herself invisible by talking about her work in these familiar and uninspiring ways. Now, during the pandemic, she needed to up-level her message.

In a brief power-session, I walked her through the essentials of my formula and how she could talk about her work in a way that touched on emotions and people's deepest desires for their lives. I also told her that she could get paid to give virtual image consultations, even during a quarantine, and charge fifteen hundred dollars for a ninety-minute session.

"No way, really?" she said.

"Yes way, really," I said.

Two weeks later, I received this email: "Marina, I just booked a client for a fifteen hundred dollar ninety-minute Zoom consultation!"

According to *Forbes*, four out of five women will fail in their business. For too many years, I was one of the four. Why? Because I was invisible.

Now, on the other side of the equation, and after having a front-row seat to women who move from the failing to the winning side of the equation, I see the path clearly.

It's about breaking through the noise with an emotional message delivered quickly—so you are seen as the powerful changemaker you are.

In our hyper-distracted, info-overloaded world, where attention spans shrink every day, the business owner who speaks to emotions first, and does so in a matter of seconds, wins.

READY TO WIN? Get a free sample of a 1-Minute Talk™ to copy and make your own PLUS a free step-by-step guide to crafting your own at www.oneminutetalkfreeoffer.com.

Marina Stamos, CEO, Marina Stamos Business Coaching, is internationally recognized as a leading women's business coach and speaker. She recovered from facedown failure to create three successful businesses and a multiple six-figure income. Her clients' successes have been featured everywhere from TEDx to *Entrepreneur* and the *Oprah Magazine*.

www.stamoscoaching.com

TO BE SEEN . . . AND HEARD!

KAREN STRAUSS

"To be seen and not heard"—that was the mantra I grew up with. My parents told my siblings and me that every time they had a party or invited adults over, we were to be good kids. When we were introduced to the adults, we were told we should smile and say, "Nice meeting you."

After that we were not to speak, and we certainly were not to utter our opinions on anything. Especially me—I was the controversial one. I always had an opinion on everything. This was not considered to be an attractive trait in a young girl. Back then, it was barely an acceptable trait in a woman.

As a result, I felt more comfortable with one-on-one conversations, and I learned to listen really well. When I grew up and went to college, people started to come to me with their issues and their problems. I was the one to give them "sage "advice. Pretty good for a nineteen-year-old!

Unfortunately, I found the same issues came up when I started working at the big corporate publishing houses. One boss told me that he didn't want to hear anything from me or how we did things at another publishing company until I had worked there for at least a year. He told me I needed to listen and learn their way of doing things before I had the right to suggest alternatives.

I found that because I was a woman, I was constantly being cut off in mid-sentence by men in the room. It was as though I did not exist, nor did I matter. Incredulously, I would bring up an idea, and no one would react to it until five minutes later when a man brought up the same idea—and then everyone said, "GREAT IDEA, TED! Brilliant!"

I thought I was hallucinating—or simply crazy. This couldn't be real. I discovered the only way to survive and thrive in a corporate setting was to put my head down, agree with the bosses, and be a "team player."

In other words, "Be invisible, and you will have a great career!"

After twelve years of putting up with this, I finally had enough. I went into business for myself, working with other small and medium-size publishing companies who needed help selling books into the large chains, wholesalers, airport stores, and wholesale clubs.

I became a freelance National Accounts Manager and consultant. A miraculous thing happened: People started listening to me. They thanked me for my input. And they paid me to be their spokesperson. What a change!

How exciting! I started to feel confident and heard for the first time in my life.

I grew my confidence by speaking out loud—but only to a small group of people in a conference room. I had not yet even begun to contemplate speaking on bigger stages to people I did not know. That terrified me.

I was very comfortable, however, advising my private clients and conducting sales seminars to larger groups, and I really enjoyed my meetings with the buyers of national chains like Barnes and Noble, Borders/Walden, Walmart, Price Club, Costco, and Hudson News Buyers.

My gift is to be able to take a complicated concept and pare it down into a thirty-second pitch. I clearly understood from the beginning that the buyer was interested in what the book was about, who the author was, who the ideal reader was, and what the marketing plan was. The buyer wanted to know if I really thought that their customers would be interested in the book.

So, these one-on-one meetings were tailor-made for me. However, this does not work so well if you are talking to hundreds of people from the stage. A thirty-second speech is not optimal if you want to leave an impression on people.

In 2010, two major events happened at the same time that significantly impacted my business and my personal life: The Borders/Walden chain closed for good, and I received a devastating diagnosis of breast cancer. With the closing of Borders/Walden, I lost 40 percent of my income (I worked on commission), and of course I could not work as well when I was going through treatments for cancer.

I had to take stock of my whole business and life. There was no way I could make up for the loss of Borders/Walden commissions, so I knew I needed to make some kind of transition.

I realized that since I was working with some independent authors already, it might be good to start my own publishing company. This coincided with an event I went to in New York City soon after my treatments were over. I attended a conference called Author101, where I met a man who ran a huge conference called The Rockstar Marketing Bootcamp. Craig Duswalt had worked for Guns and Roses and Air Supply, and he applied his lessons from the music world to helping entrepreneurs think outside the box so they could grow their businesses.

Craig invited me to his conference in California, and it changed my life! There were five hundred people in the room—all entrepreneurs in various phases of their business or aspiring entrepreneurs who had full-time jobs but were getting ready to take the leap.

When Craig started teaching that writing a book was essential to establishing your credibility in your niche and how it helped you stand out from the crowd, I knew I had found my group! I was all in!

I joined Craig's mastermind and quickly became known as the publishing expert. Within a short amount of time, Craig and I created a publishing company called The Rockstar Publishing House. The year we rolled it out, I got to speak live in front of six hundred people. Speaking about a subject that is near and dear to my heart was one of the most exhilarating hours of my life. I have worked in publishing my whole adult life, so I knew what I was talking about. And to see such interest in the eyes of the people in the audience and feel the engagement that was happening in the room was such a thrill! The hope, the smiles, the anticipation on the faces of these people gave me chills. To think I had that impact on them! My words mattered. My promises to them mattered. I was going to help them write, publish, and promote their first book!

It truly filled me with purpose. I was able to offer something tangible to a large group of people, not just one-on-one anymore.

This changed the projection of my professional life moving forward.

I began to find other partners to joint venture with, eventually working with organizations such as the Women Speakers Association; Mark Porteous' group, the Soul Affiliate Alliance; Suzanne Evans of Driven Inc; and Dannella Burnett, an event planner and organizer of the group Speakers Need to Speak.

I had the opportunity to speak on all their stages and guide people through the writing process. I helped them learn how to develop the big idea for their book, and answer questions such as: Who is the ideal reader? Who is NOT the ideal reader? What is the outcome you most want to achieve with your book? (Possible answers include becoming known as the expert in your niche, becoming more visible by speaking on more stages, or being interviewed on radio and podcasts, and having influencers write about you and your book.) I showed them how authoring a book could increase their income by gaining new clients, or perhaps be used as a stepping-stone to create other products: a course, a workbook, or maybe even a whole coaching program.

As I began to speak (at first live—and now virtually), I have been able to reach thousands of people. Many people have booked appointments with me because they either had a book already in mind or were inspired by my words and felt compelled to act on the dream of writing a book.

You might not realize that writing a book helps you get on more stages—it helps you to be seen and heard. I find it so rewarding to reach so many people at once and hear them tell me that I've inspired them to take action. Some people actually thank me in the acknowledgment section of their book . . . the idea of me being able to have so much impact in another person's life is a dream come true—and the biggest honor I can think of. Even better than a standing ovation!

Karen Strauss is a speaker, book coach, and author, with more than thirty-five years in the publishing industry. As the founder of Hybrid Global Publishing, she works with speakers, authors, and entrepreneurs to write, publish, distribute, and promote their books in order to generate unlimited leads, get on more speaking stages, and grow their business by attracting more clients.

www.hybridglobalpublishing.com

WHEN WOULD YOU WANT TO KNOW?

CHARLES THEISEN

What if something you thought to be true about your retirement plan, taxes, and future financial planning turned out not to be true—when would you want to know that?

I've asked that question from the stage to thousands of people, and they all give me the same answer: NOW!

Have you ever wondered what it would feel like to work with a "team" of financial professionals—not just one or two, but an entire team—and as a result, know beyond the shadow of a doubt that your financial future is secure, free from over-paying taxes, and protected from any litigation?

Have you ever wondered what it would be like to be able to maximize your lifestyle today instead of cutting back on your lifestyle in an effort to save more money for retirement—and still build a legacy that you could pass on tax-free to your loved ones?

Have you ever wondered what it would be like to wake up with more time, money, and energy than you thought possible?

I've asked those three questions as well from the stage to thousands of people. Many say they have wondered; however, they also say they have no idea how to make any of that happen—and neither did I at one point in my life.

Today I am the creator of the Wealth and Freedom "Empowerment" System. My goal is for my clients to find out what they don't know—in other words, all the Golden Nuggets and secrets of wealth I have learned over the last fifteen years of shadowing and networking with the best tax

masters, CPAs, EAs, tax lawyers, financial advisors, insurance professionals, IRA specialists, and trust attorneys.

Most of my clients share with me that they feel confused, they've
lost money because they chose the wrong investment or instrument, and
unfortunately, they've also been taken advantage of by so-called financial
professionals.

"I know how you feel," I tell them. "I felt the same way years ago."

And then I share with them the Golden Nuggets I have learned.
The result? They learn the whole truth about how many options they
really have to live the life of their dreams on their terms, not at the
mercy of the US government or any other institution. I show them how
to be prepared to take action, build their legacy, and be extraordinarily
confident in planning their financial future. They learn how to be in
control.

As you are about to read, I had to start over financially at fifty-six.
It wasn't the result of irresponsible behavior, or mismanaged risk, or any
fault of my own.

Life happened. My wife was diagnosed with a second primary form
of cancer.

The only medical facility we felt could help her win the battle with
dignity was in Tulsa, Oklahoma. We lived in Fort Lauderdale, Florida.
We were in Tulsa on and off for two to six weeks at a time for three years.
In total I devoted 26,280 hours as her 24/7 patient advocate and caregiver.

I do not say that to impress you, but rather to impress upon you: Life
happens. *You had better be ready. It can be unrelenting.*

We sold everything we had, including our home, and emptied our
retirement accounts. I held nothing back to give her a shot at beating the
cancer and have quality of life in the process.

We fought together for three years. She had her homegoing in
December 2008. I was devastated. My wife was gone.

***To add insult to injury, I soon found out that had I known then what
I know and teach now about money, I would not have needed to suffer
financial devastation as well as the loss of my wife.***

After her loss, I responded with a vengeance. I was determined to
educate myself and restore my family financially in the least amount
of time so I would never have to go through something like this again.

My experience as my wife's patient advocate and caregiver required unwavering awareness. Financial peace of mind is no different. You must be proactive and ask questions. Never assume or accept only one opinion.

I created a SAFE Environment for myself, where I would not make financial decisions without getting a second and then a third opinion. I asked an annoying amount of questions, shadowed the best of the best in the industry, and eventually became a licensed life insurance tax professional.

It worked. I discovered the Tax Secrets of the Rich.

I found out there were dozens of strategies my professionals had never told me because they did not know them or had never been trained to utilize them.

It wasn't their fault. The "traditional" model of financial planning is that every professional is a specialist, but there is no communication between them and their clients. They grow your portfolio, take a 4 percent withdrawal, and hope you don't run out of money before you run out of breath.

What secrets did I discover that you would love to know? Allow me to share a few examples. Banks and the elite wealthy purchase billions of dollars in cash-value life insurance for zero-loss provisions, tax-free accumulation and distribution, and leverage by borrowing against their cash value with unstructured payment options.

Banks will finance your retirement account, doubling your retirement income; this is called premium financing. Super 401Ks allow for the tax deferral of hundreds of thousands of dollars, "defined" benefit plans that "guarantee" a specific income, and unlimited funding in case you need to catch up on savings and have the means to do so.

Accelerated "critical illness" benefits, including heart attack, stroke, and cancer, allow 70 percent distribution of your life insurance NOW, when you need the funds the most! Less than twenty companies out of thousands offer this.

My friends, there are so many more secrets I am ready, willing, and able to teach you so you, your family, and your business are prepared for both good and bad times.

I have identified dedicated professionals who meet my standard of providing holistic care for those clients who choose to implement my chosen strategies. I provide ALL of these secrets and more in a safe, no pressure environment.

What Do We Know?

We know what we have been taught and or conditioned to believe! We're familiar with terms like *Wall Street, 401K, IRA,* and maybe a few other accounts everyone else uses. Well, I've found out that there many other options available to you and me. I've discovered what I call the "Whole Truth."

The typical focus when it comes to financial planning is to GROW your money. But there is very little emphasis or education on how to KEEP your money and GROW it TAX-FREE, let alone LEVERAGE it to create cash flow.

We are willing to embrace risk, growth, and working harder to "make" more money because we are not aware there is any other way. This is often NOT good for our health. What good is the money if we are not healthy enough to enjoy it?

We also know to run the other way when we see a life insurance professional. Just kidding—but it's true; just ask anyone. But before we throw them under the bus, let's recognize that they are doing the best they can, and most of them have noble intentions.

The problem I found, though, is that while life insurance is THE MOST widely used and complex instrument employed by the wealthy for tax mitigation and estate planning, very few agents understand it. I had to self-educate and associate with tax masters and insurance industry geniuses to fully understand its power.

It's Time—The World Needs to Know

Some of you might be saying, "It's too late for me."

I say, "It's not."

I will share with you dozens of proven strategies to give you peace of mind, with no one offering to "sell" a product. What a relief, right? You relax, learn, see a brighter future, and no pressure!

First, you will become self-educated financially.

Second, you will be better equipped to choose what professionals you want to work with because you will know how to select them. You will live your life on your terms—no one else's.

Third, you will experience more time, money, energy, and freedom in your life, because you will have solved the two biggest problems you will ever have as a person or business: namely, taxes and litigation.

The quality of your life depends upon the quality of the questions that you ask—*and don't ask.* Learn what to ask. I'm sure you are familiar with an FAQ list. But have you ever seen an FUAQ list? Of course not. *Frequently **UN**-Asked Questions.* I had to learn the hard way that what I didn't know would hurt me, that when I did not know what I did not know, mistakes happen. You must be alert and get all the facts now. Why?

Mistakes are dangerous. Taxes are increasing and not knowing the tax rate on your tax-deferred money is dangerous.

We cannot afford not to know the rules we will be subject to tax-wise that could decimate our retirement accounts.

I am concerned for you and your health and wealth. That's why I am so passionate about sharing my Golden Nuggets with you and the world before it's too late. You and the world need to know!

Charles Theisen is a sought-after speaker and wealth strategist who has been in the industry for nearly two decades. His business philosophy is "own nothing and control everything," which he shares through his unique tax-saving structures and strategies.

www.charlestheisen360.com

YOU HAVE SOMETHING
TO SAY

ABIGAIL TIEFENTHALER

I never wanted to be on stage. Oh, I definitely had plenty to say, but I preferred the intimacy of sharing my stories behind the scenes with anyone who would listen.

It may have had something to do with the saying "Be seen but not heard." I'm not really sure why my mother said this to me more than once as a girl. I think it was the result of the exhaustive questions and suggestions I would offer on any topic. I always had a perspective.

As I moved up in my career, I had plenty to say, but I didn't have a seat at the table. I was one of the people in the room but without a voice. I could give recommendations behind the scenes, but they were shared with clients by my management. Imagine the badgering my management had to endure so I could get my thoughts out!

You see, I'm a problem solver. Always have been. I see things and usually know how to fix them, or at least provide a possible solution. As a business and brand strategist, it is an excellent gift to have, but as a young child, or someone climbing the corporate ladder, not so much. Especially as a woman. And while friends, family, and some of my managers found it cute or spunky, it eventually became tiresome to my supporters. I think that's why I always felt like a bull in a china shop during my fifteen years in corporate America—and why I eventually found my place as an entrepreneur.

But speaking in large groups intimidated me. When I finally found a small, women-owned marketing agency that encouraged my ideas and supported my recommendations, it still was hard to take the lead because I wasn't comfortable being in that position of authority. I let others fill that position. During one agency presentation to a prospective client that I brought to the agency, I was supposed to lead the meeting. During our rehearsals I kept minimizing my role until basically I was only introducing the agency team. I was so flummoxed that I gave my senior management various parts of the meeting to present.

But something interesting happened once we were at the prospective clients' offices. When seated, I was able to do all the transitions and recommendations that go into an agency presentation. My bosses didn't stop me as they saw I was managing the meeting successfully, so I kept going. By the end of the meeting, I knew we had won the account. More importantly, I knew I had beaten my fear about presenting to a larger group.

I realized that while standing in front of crowds was still terrifying, speaking to a group was okay if we were all on the same level. I built authority and credibility through my knowledge instead of an imposing stance. It was an amazing revelation.

One step forward for sure, but still, the idea of speaking to large groups terrified me—sitting or standing. It was a self-worth thing. What if I shared my expertise with others and they didn't agree? Or didn't think I was saying anything important? What if my audience got bored?

Speaking one-to-one and to small groups gave me the opportunity to read the room, get an idea of where attendees stood on an issue, and gauge their level of interest. I could adapt as the conversation went on.

I couldn't do that speaking to crowds. And what a talker hates most is not having someone listen to them. Add that to someone who's careful about being taken seriously and well . . . speaking on stages was still a no-go for me. Why even consider it as there are so many branding experts out there already? What was I going to add to the conversation?

To make matters worse, when I get nervous, my thoughts get jumbled, and I speak too fast. How could I communicate to increase understanding, inspire, or compel? And I can get blotchy, too, so everything that's coming up on the inside shows on the outside.

So I got really good at communicating one-on-one or in small groups. However, as I honed my strategic skills and branding successes, I was asked to share my stories and ideas with bigger groups. The idea petrified me. For years I ignored the invites.

Deep inside I knew I had a message to share, something unique that people searching for branding and marketing answers needed to hear. I grew up in the branding and marketing industry. My degree is in marketing. My fifteen years in corporate were in marketing, and my twenty-four-plus years as a businessowner has revolved around marketing. My skills are both wide and deep. I often say that if there is someone with more marketing experience than I have, I want to meet them. I also can't turn off my need to help people make better marketing decisions. My brain just doesn't stop.

Speaking to larger audiences was a critical growth edge for me, and I knew it. In 2010, after co-founding a women's business networking group, the other three women asked me to run the meetings. With anywhere from twenty-five to forty-five women in attendance, my job was to welcome, update, and introduce the speaker. I became the face of the meeting. At our five-year anniversary, I thanked the members who had been patient with me as I took baby steps to get comfortable speaking to bigger groups. Running this group made me the speaker I am today.

In 2014 I was invited to be a speaker at a women's conference. With more than one hundred in attendance, I had an opportunity to make an offer. I was scared and excited at the same time. I worked with a coach to help me create a signature presentation. I spent all my free time watching videos of speakers. I noticed what they wore. How they walked the stage. How they spoke. I was obsessed with showing up professionally and being relatable. I even got a spray tan and hired someone to do my hair and makeup. I was ready for my Saturday afternoon slot.

And then it happened. The event organizer asked if I could switch my time to Sunday morning because one of the Sunday speakers had to leave early. Being a team player, I said yes. I thought this would work to my advantage. And it did. The woman who had done my hair and makeup came back on Sunday. The organizer introduced me with a very enthusiastic and supportive introduction. I made an offer, and twenty-three women eventually said "yes"! How I got them there is another story!

Since then I've spoken on multiple stages, both live and virtually. I've spoken at conferences, networking events, summits, and on podcasts. I've spoken to teach, inspire, and sell. Event organizers ask me to share their stage because I'm real. I'm transparent. And I will always share my best practices. Plus, I support my event organizers. I found that when you support them, they support you.

While I don't ever think anyone masters speaking, any more than they master marketing or sales, I have been able to learn and apply key fundamentals to become a popular guest speaker. The following principles work live or virtually.

First, remember that a great presentation should feel like a conversation between friends, so get good at communicating one-on-one. Good communication skills are foundational to every great speaker. Learn to read and respond to your audience. This allows you to adapt your presentation authentically.

Second, do the work to prepare for every speaking opportunity, even if you're using the same presentation. Be all in. Every event is unique. Every audience is unique. Don't let your audience down.

Third, get support where you need it. Nothing replaces confidence when you have support and know you are prepared. Your audience will see your effort. You will appreciate your success. And stay around during an event, virtual or live.

Fourth, make it easy for your audience to connect with you during or after an event. Invite them to download a free gift. Give them a reason to come into your world.

Finally, be excited to step on that stage, live or otherwise. Enthusiasm goes a long way. People respond more to how you're saying something than to what you're saying. Staying fresh enables you to continue growing and learning as you sharpen your message.

If you are alive, you have a story. Find your voice. The sooner you learn how to use it in a way that feels right to you, the faster you'll be able to create the impact most speakers seek.

Do I consider myself a speaker? No. I still define myself as a problem solver who has an important message to share, and speaking is one of the ways I meet new audiences that need to hear it. Whatever you want to do, find a way—because your message is important, and the world needs to hear it.

Known as the "Launch and Leverage Strategist," **Abigail Tiefenthaler** is the co-founder of LMS, a marketing services agency that works with professional coaches who are ready to make six and seven figures consistently. LMS brings the best of brand strategy and marketing implementation so clients can go from practitioners to businessowners.

www.launchesmadesimple.com

THE PRICE OF SHOWING UP
TO PLAY THE GAME

VICTOR R. VENTO

I turned the corner and thought, *Holy crap! I don't belong here—these people are way more successful than I am.*

How did I even get here?

A few weeks before, one of my clients was talking about an upcoming sponsorship. She mentioned that it was going to be a big one and suggested that I attend. So I agreed to join in on a webinar that the event host had scheduled before the event.

It was about ninety minutes long, and some of the things she was talking about resonated with me. She even had a contest going on at the end of the webinar. She mentioned that the winner would win a sponsorship to the event. Of course that caught my attention.

You see, I come from the online space, and attention is everything. If you can't get attention, you lose the game.

I have a game I play every time I show up online to win. It has four phases to it, which we'll get to a bit later in this chapter.

I wasn't familiar with event sponsorships or speaking on stages because what I usually did was to set up attention-grabbing ads to generate L.E.A.D.S. (an acronym for people who say Let's Engage And Do Something). I would start conversations, build relationships, and invite those relationships to scale their business.

I know how to win online, but this event sponsorship and speaking on stage world was new to me back then, and I had no idea what I was getting myself into. But like most successful entrepreneurs and business owners, I decided to Play The Game. I joined the contest and crafted a one-minute speech right then and there. After they tallied the scores, the team came back and said it was close because it was almost a tie between first and second place.

The event host said that these two people had the most powerful messages and had showed up as the most authentic version of themselves.

The good news is that I was one of these two people. I definitely 100 percent had lost.

Why is that good news? Because I wouldn't have had any collateral for a sponsorship booth, and I was definitely not at that level . . . yet. Instead I purchased a VIP ticket to the event so that I could play the game again, and this time I would play the game that I already had an advantage in, and I would adapt the rules to this in-person event.

With my VIP ticket, I was entered into another contest where I had a chance to be onstage and speak to an audience of about three hundred people. I confidently stood in front of the judges in the back of the room, passed out my score form to each of them, and shared the four phases I use online to get epic results.

Phase 1: *Attract* the attention of your audience with an opening story hook that breaks the ice.

Phase 2: *Engage* them with a story that keeps their attention and creates momentum for them to naturally progress through it.

Phase 3: *Elevate* them from the lows to the highs of your story so they can find themselves in it and continue to progress and evolve themselves.

Phase 4: . . .

"**TIME!**" said one of the judges.

Cliffhanger, I know . . .

My message resonated; I started to build a relationship because I showed up authentically as myself. I left them wanting more, which is always the goal, but I did it unintentionally because I ran out of time.

The judges gave me my scores and . . . I didn't win . . . again.

It's okay, though, because I stepped out of my comfort zone. I'm way more comfortable behind the scenes than I am in front of the stage, but I wasn't going to let that stop me from playing the game. I went back to my room after registration ended and devised another path to take that stage.

The next day, while the host was teaching everyone how to grow your business, she provided several opportunities to walk up to a mic and ask questions. Most of us seemed to be terrified of walking up to the mic and showing up authentically.

I saw this as an opportunity to get access to this business coach, so I walked up, introduced myself and my marketing agency, and asked my questions. I was raw and real about where I was and where I wanted to go. Because of how authentic I was, attendees wanted to have a chat with me, and even the sponsors knew who I was. Seriously, I usually have to pay for this type of attention.

Naturally, as the day progressed, I was becoming known as the event celebrity who was courageous enough to show up and "BE SEEN" (which funny enough was the main theme of this event). I made my own stage, and I **attracted** a lot of people, **engaged** with them, and provided insight so they too could **elevate** themselves and their business.

Before the first day ended, the event host made one final invitation to step up to the mic and ask her anything. What do you think I did? I walked up and asked, "How do I get up on that stage?"

She paused . . . and then said that all the spots were already taken, but that I could become a sponsor if I wanted stage time.

Ouch! I hadn't struck out that many times since . . . well, I'll save that for another day.

Even though I couldn't get up on that stage to speak to the audience on my topic and message, I wasn't going to accept that as my reality. *Maybe not this time*, I thought to myself, *but next time I'll get up onstage to share my message.*

I think that one of the reasons most people resonated with what I was asking was because I became the voice inside their head. I was asking the questions most of them were too afraid to ask themselves. Showing up authentically allowed me to resonate with most of the attendees.

On day two, I continued the conversations I began the previous day with people. But after lunch, as we were all getting ready to head back in for the next session, a member of the staff approached me. And I felt a little worried. *Oh crap, was I talking too much? Was I being too loud? Did I do something wrong?*

I think most of us feel that way on the inside. Am I too much? Am I too loud? Am I enough?

I expected to be asked to leave, even though there wasn't any reason to think that way.

In fact, the opposite was true. This particular staff member said, "Can you come with me for a second?" She actually invited me backstage to speak with the event host because of how much I had showed up and continuously asked the questions I knew everyone else had.

The event host said, "We want to invite you to be part of our panel segment."

At that point, I was ecstatic. "Wow! You want to invite *me* to be on the panel?"

And that's where I began this chapter. I turned the corner and thought *Holy crap! I don't belong here—these people are way more successful than I am.*

But then I thought, *Except I do belong here.* The theme of the event was *Be Seen,* and you can only do that when you show up to play the game. And I had showed up to play.

What do you think happened next? When I walked out on that stage, everyone cheered. They clapped because everyone knew who I was. I'd had at least two conversations with the majority of the people in that room. All because of how I play the game . . .

That event led to a few things. One of the most impactful was a five-times growth in my business. It led to hundreds of potential ideal prospects *and* a client relationship with the event host. Now, what's the lesson here?

Let's close the loop on that cliffhanger earlier.

This is exactly what I do online. All the time I show up, and I play the game. I followed my four phases to Generate Never-Ending L.E.A.D.S.:

Phase 1: *Attract* the attention of your audience.

Phase 2: *Engage* them and create momentum for them.

Phase 3: *Elevate* them from the lows to the highs so they can find themselves and naturally progress and evolve.

Phase 4: *Convert* by inviting them to go even faster and get support.

Because I showed up to play the game, I can attribute about thirty-four thousand dollars to that event—as well as my first stage—because most attendees opted into my freebie.

Coaches, experts, and service-based business owners turn to **Victor R. Vento** to help them show up authentically and resonate with their ideal followers so they can profitably scale their business at will with paid traffic. Visit his website to learn more.

www.workwithvic.com